T0135621

Dissertation

Functional Web Site Specification

Torsten Gipp

Universität Koblenz-Landau

Bibliografische Information Der Deutschen Bibliothek

Die Deutsche Bibliothek verzeichnet diese Publikation in der Deutschen
Nationalbibliografie; detaillierte bibliografische Daten sind im Internet über
http://dnb.ddb.de abrufbar.

ISBN 3-8325-1271-3

Logos Verlag Berlin
Comeniushof, Gubener Str. 47,
10243 Berlin
Tel.: +49 030 42 85 10 90
Fax: +49 030 42 85 10 92
INTERNET: http://www.logos-verlag.de

Abstract

Web sites are inherently complex software artefacts whose specification, creation, and maintenance is everything but trivial. Using *models* to capture relevant aspects of a web site is an established way to master the complexity. The models are well-defined abstract views on a web site, and they can be used to *describe* the web site and also to automatically *generate* it. This holds especially when the models are sufficiently formal.

This text shows that *functional programming languages* are concise and powerful formalisms that are perfectly suited to specify a great number of the identified aspects. Thus, we employ functional programs as models for selected web site aspects. These functional *specifications* are executable and they are used by the run-time system to actually drive the web site. This approach yields a distinguished set of benefits, e.g., the consistency of the specification with the end product, high expressive power of the specifications, the facilitation of testing and simulation, and the possibility to incorporate existing tools and technologies to provide specific 'features' like configuration management. The ideas are general enough to provide that the realisation is not constrained to a particular functional programming language or a particular run-time system.

The applicability of the approach is illustrated by referring to two example projects during the introduction of the necessary models. The models themselves are identified after considering the current state of the literature and by applying strict separation of concerns. Apart from the incorporation of a functional programming language into the world of web site modelling, the main focus of this text will be the description of the models and, in particular, their *integration*.

Zusammenfassung (German Abstract)

Webpräsenzen (web sites) sind komplexe Artefakte der Softwareerstellung, und ihre Spezifikation, Erzeugung und Pflege ist ein anspruchsvolles Unterfangen. Ein vielbeschrittener Weg zur Reduktion der Komplexität ist die Verwendung von *Modellen* zur Abbildung relevanter Aspekte einer Webpräsenz. Die Modelle sind wohl-definierte Abstraktionen und können sowohl zur *Beschreibung* als auch zur automatisierten *Generierung* von Webpräsenzen herangezogen werden. Dies gilt umso mehr, je formaler die Modelle sind.

Der vorliegende Text enthüllt *funktionale Programmiersprachen* als einen konzisen und ausdrucksstarken Formalismus zur Repräsentation einer großen Zahl der angesprochenen Aspekte. Die Modelle werden also in Form von funktionalen Programmen repräsentiert. Diese funktionalen *Spezifikationen* sind ausführbar und das Laufzeitsystem kann sie direkt verwenden, um die eigentliche Webpräsenz zum Leben zu erwecken. Dieser Ansatz offenbart eine Reihe von Vorteilen, wie beispielsweise die Konsistenz der Spezifikation mit dem tatsächlichen Produkt, eine große Ausdruckskraft der Spezifikationen, die Erleichterung von Test und Simulation, sowie die Möglichkeit zur Integration externer Tools und Technologien, um z.B. Funktionalitäten wie 'Konfigurationsmanagement' zu realisieren. Die vorgestellten Ideen sind allgemein und richten sich nicht an spezifische Laufzeitsysteme oder eine spezifische funktionale Programmiersprache.

Die Umsetzbarkeit des Ansatzes wird durch zwei Beispielanwendungen demonstriert, die während der Vorstellung der nötigen Modelle herangezogen werden. Die Modelle wiederum werden durch Aufarbeitung des aktuellen Forschungsstands und durch Einhaltung einer Disziplin der 'Trennung der Belange' identifiziert. Neben der Verwendung einer funktionalen Programmiersprache zur Modellierung von Webpräsenzen liegt der Schwerpunkt dieser Arbeit auf der Beschreibung der einzelnen Modelle und, insbesondere, ihrer *Integration*.

Prelude

I always wondered why many books – and PhD theses in particular – had a preface that alluded to a mental exhaustion of the author, contained words of thanks to beloved people who allegedly helped constrain the physical sufferance to a level that was at least bearable, or expressions of gratefulness for the final termination of a constant strain that had almost succeeded in driving the pitiable text-producer out of his mind. Creating a work of this magnitude was, it seemed, just this: painful. Was it exaggeration?

Paradoxically, the same prefaces also reported on episodes of pure and delightful inspiration, on stimulating situations where mountain tops were finally reached, and on breathtaking views that more than rewarded for the – then – seemingly insignificant efforts of the climb. Did these moments of success really alleviate, or even compensate for, the previous sufferings?

What could make a person write things like that? How profoundly affective must have been the experiences that evoked such feelings?

What had these authors gone through?

I do know now.

Prelude

Foreword

This text is one, or better *the*, result of my working at the Institute for Software Technology at Koblenz-Landau University. It is the materialised outcome of my time as a research assistant in the working group of Prof. Dr. Jürgen Ebert, who also heads the Software Technology Institute. Under his auspices I conducted my work, and I have learned much from him.

In the course of my assistantship, the initial plans set out for my dissertation underwent quite some adjustments, some of minor, some of major impact. I think this is positive, since a project like this should be allowed to evolve, to ripen like a fruit. Now, it is time to harvest the yield.

Acknowledgements

A PhD thesis is the work of one single person, and this text is no exception. Nevertheless, this does not imply that there is nobody to be grateful to – in the contrary. Firstly, a PhD thesis is a *scientific* work, and as such it draws from many sources, and builds on the contributions and achievements of fellow scientists. They are paid due credit by citing their works and pointing out their findings and results. Secondly, a PhD thesis is a piece of work that takes quite some time to create, and in the course of this time is influenced, directed, redirected, bashed, smashed, and praised by many. Constructive criticism is the engine that keeps the vehicle going. I thank all those who gave advice or any other flavour of feedback. *Any* input was valuable, and has contributed to the overall result.

In particular, I wish to express my warmest thanks to my mentor, Prof. Dr. Jürgen Ebert, for his endurance, kindness, and his unshakeable goodwill. Although being continually smothered with a workload that would be enough to keep two or three further 'instances' of himself busy around the clock (alas, however, they have not shown up so far), he always found the time for a talk. I appreciate the scheme of work of having regular meetings, so as to keep each other up to date, and to get immediate feedback and fresh input. I had every support I could have wished for.

Prof. Dr. Gerti Kappel, who heads the Business Informatics Group in the Institute for Software Technology and Interactive Systems at the Vienna University of Technology, agreed to dedicate a significant amount of her time for learning what my thesis was all about and for writing her statement on my work. She and her group did also provide very valuable feedback, for which I am particularly thankful.

I will restrain from listing further names of colleagues, friends, relatives, or other people whom I wish to express my thankfulness to. This is not only to avoid the inexcusable and embarrassing error of forgetting to mention somebody who should have been mentioned, or of including somebody who should not have; not to speak of the necessity to argue about the particular *order* of any such listing, which is commonly avoided by the killer argument that an *alphabetical* order be sufficiently neutral, which of course it is not. Anyhow: those individuals who *did* contribute, to which amount whatsoever, already know of my gratefulness. It is at least questionable whether finding one's name printed near the end of the foreword to this work is apt to compensate or reward for the rendered help, or whether it is just ludicrous or even annoying. Personally, I do not think that being mentioned here is an honour, or at least not a sufficiently high one, and it is nothing less than the highest praise that these people deserve.

So I can only say this to you: I am very fond of you guys, and you know that!

Contents

Contents

14 Executable Web Page Specifications   157

15 Definitions   165

Part I

Introduction

On Making Good Web Sites

'You want a web site? No problem. Use your favourite text editor, have a brief look into the HTML specification, and there you go.

You want to present up-to-date data that resides in a relational database management system? There is CGI, use that!

Your web site starts to get complex? There are broken links? HTML and image files that seem not to belong to the web site anymore, but you do not know for sure? You are not the only person working on that web site, and the others keep messing up the structure you devised? Perhaps you should consider a web content management system! Already did? Too expensive? Well, some sacrifices are necessary.

Bought it? Now what? You want an on-line shop system? That is easy: just tick that check box in the configuration screen labelled "enable on-line shop system." Isn't that nice?

You want to change the colour of the product description inside the entry form? Sorry, that is not possible. Please buy another web content management system.'

Web sites underwent a dramatic evolution during the past years. The complexity of modern web sites is astoundingly impressive, and it has long become clear that the manual creation and maintenance of single HTML files is out of the question. Software tools are needed that allow for the successful mastering of large web sites. But how do they work? Which tasks do they perform, and how do they do it? Which solutions are at hand to solve the eminent problems of creation and maintenance, how do they compare, and how could they be improved?

These and more questions almost instantaneously unfold when thinking about web sites, and they are the inspirational source for this work. In order to lay down what this work is all about, section 1.1 shall clarify the scope. Section 1.2 will focus on the concrete goal that is to be reached inside this scope. The last section of this introductory chapter, section 1.3, shall give a coarse outline of the text that will follow in the subsequent chapters.

1.1 Scope

This text is about *functional web site specification*. A *web site* is a coherent and related collection of *resources*◇[1], typically including one distinguished resource (home page) acting as an entry point into the collection. A *resource*, in its broadest sense, is 'anything that has identity' ([BLFIM98]). We can temporarily interpret it as being synonymous to *electronic document* at this point. The term 'site' does not refer to the geographical location of the resources on a specific server machine. Rather, the whole site may be spread over any number of physical servers. As pointed out in [Tec03], the term *web presence*, often used synonymous to web site, seems to fit more properly, stressing the fact that the visitor is experiencing a virtual presence rather than stepping into a physically existing place. However, the term *web site* is used more commonly, so it is the one that will be used throughout this text.

The resources that form a web site, and accordingly the web site as a whole, are software artefacts. Viewing from some distance, we can characterise a web site as a software application, but one that is delivered to the users by the means of web technology. There is a great number of similarities between web applications and 'traditional' software applications, which results in the idea that the creation of web sites involves the same, or at least comparable, techniques, methods and approaches commonly subsumed by *software engineering*. However, there is good reason to regard *web engineering*◇ as a discipline in its own right, as there are many specific challenges to be mastered, e.g., the integration of hypertexts. But much that has proven beneficial in traditional software engineering can be applied for web engineering as well. One pivotal idea of this category is modelling and specification.

A *model* is a 'simplified description of a system used in explanations, calculations, etc.' [Hor89, model (n) 3]. A model is an abstraction that is precise enough to describe what the desired result should comprise of. In order to highlight the precision and conciseness, we call these models *specifications*.

We regard web sites as artefacts that can be described in a formal, preferably mathematical way, so that the descriptions can be used as a basis for communication between the participants of the development process. The clear advantage of specifications is that this communication takes place in the knowing that each communication partner has exactly the same understanding of the conveyed meanings and the corresponding implications. Furthermore, these descriptions serve as specifications of parts of the end product, which makes them authoritative sources that *define* the actual web site, or respective parts of it.

Yet another advantage is given by this precision: specifications with a well-defined semantics can be translated and interpreted systematically, i.e., by a software tool. This offers the possibility to *execute* the specifications, which is a very high value as it manifests the coherence between the specification and the implementation of the end product. It is one of the most important goals of software engineering to give advice on how to produce software that is essentially equivalent, or at least infinitesimally close to, its description.

---

[1] The symbol ◇ marks a word as being defined in the glossary (see page 165).

We also commit ourselves to this goal, and we will try to specify web sites as formal as possible.

In this light, it is promising to look into directions that are not always in the centre of common consideration, one of which is the area of functional languages. They provide for formal, powerful, abstract and concise specifications, and allow to introduce any amount of additional levels of abstractions. These properties make them particularly useful for modelling web sites.

The adjective *functional*◇ has at least three different meanings (cf. [Oxf05, functional (adj.)]). Firstly, it can be used synonymously to *utilitarian*, which signifies that something is (just) practical, useful, without any particular decoration. Secondly, something may be called functional when it has a special purpose, and when it makes something else possible or enables it, e.g., when something plays a pivotal role in some process. Thirdly, especially when talking about a machine or an organisation or a system, being 'functional' means to be working, or able to work.

All three meanings fit perfectly for conveying the intent behind using *functional* web site specifications: they *are* practical and useful, without any unnecessary embellishments; they *do* serve a particular purpose, because they *define* the web site; and they are also *working* in the sense that can be executed to drive the web site.

Finally, of course, it must be pointed out that the term *functional* has a special meaning in mathematics and computer science, namely: referring to mathematical functions and their application. And *this* particular connotation of this term is what lies behind our specification on the technical level. Not only are they *functional* in the sense shown by the three meanings, but they are *functions* as well.

The title of this work, 'functional web site specification,' could also have read *functional web site specifications* (note the final 's'). The second version focusses on the *artefacts*◇ that are produced, while the first one takes a somewhat broader view and encompasses the whole *process* of specification, as well as its results. We chose this version in favour of the other one because we wish to tackle both kinds of problems: how does one proceed?, and which artefacts does it require to do so?

1.2 Goal

This work presents a means to specify web sites. Suggestions are made that involve the creation of functional specifications which serve as models for specifically identified *aspects*◇ of web sites, e.g., the web site's content, the hypertext structure, and the dynamics of the site. These models are integrated to result in a coherent view on a web site in question, allowing for the implementation of the desired end product. The web sites thus specified have, *due* to their being specified and due to the *way* in which this is done, a number of positive properties. One of these is their good level of maintainability.

This work provides a coherent and integrated set of models for the description of web sites. The models will focus on well-defined aspects of web sites, and the identification of the aspects is achieved by applying strict separation of concerns. The models, as software engineering artefacts, can be subjected to established software engineering techniques, which provides for utmost flexibility and re-use of existing knowledge.

The findings presented herein are profound enough to serve as a groundwork for further involvement. Since we are working on fairly new ground, and on a rather low level, one should not expect to see any finished skyscrapers yet. We do not claim to having found the silver bullet that solves all open issues. Rather, we try to point towards a different way of thinking and to an employment of tools, in this case, functional specifications, that have not yet been tried intensively for this particular endeavour. Our work shows that these tools do serve very well, and that new possibilities are opened by relying on them.

Thus, is should be pointed out that having shown the successful application of functional languages does not render other approaches useless. In the contrary: we see our approach as an extension to the concert of existing approaches. Our ideas can be used by others, in the same way as we rely on techniques that are already documented in current literature. It is our intended goal to become and stay aware of the whole breadth of the field we are working in, its vast dimensions notwithstanding.

Describing software artefacts involves the employment of a sound terminology. Eventually, there must be given a taxonomy of terms, so that one can talk about the problem domain without taking the risk of getting lost in the mist of ambiguity and misunderstanding. Searching for these definitions results in a broad overview of the area in question. At some point, there will rise a need to stop going any further, because the sheer number of ramifying trunks of questions will lead to no end. Then, it must be carefully decided which direction to take and which path not to pursue.

We do not want to start from scratch, as far as the aspects are concerned that have to be considered when describing a web site. While our aim is to identify these aspects by looking at existing web sites, we base our descriptions on existing knowledge in web site modelling. Therefore, before presenting the actual web site models, we will start by introducing a structure that is, according to the current state of literature, accepted as being appropriate for this task.

When this step is reached, we will *apply* the findings to a real application. A good way to prove that one knows how to do something is to actually do it. In order to arrive at a generic modelling approach for a web site, it is fruitful to look at specific web sites and to make a model for them. With this as a basis, it is possible to identify common aspects and thus complete one's knowledge of a common model and its constituents.

One of the main contributions of this work is the idea of using a *functional language* to describe and specify a web site's structure and the structure of the different pages. The functional specifications are executable and they are directly used by the run-time system to drive the web site.

The specifications are written in a functional programming language, being very well suited to formally define abstract data types and corresponding functions that act upon them. Since we regard web pages as functions, using a functional programming language to write them down is an almost natural choice. As we shall see, the definitions are inherently concise and easy to understand.

We aim at, and presumably succeeded in, providing an approach that is powerful, open, and extensible. This aim influences many decisions, and we will always refrain from choosing paths that might confine or constrain the solution we are about to construct. As an example, the functional programming language that will be employed in order to show how the specification actually look like, Haskell, is chosen because of its widespread use, good tool support and the overwhelming number of available extensions. However, we do not prescribe this language in particular, and it only serves to demonstrate our findings and to show off that the approach works. Using a different language should not impose any principal problems.

In this spirit, the following text will deliver the description of a coherent approach, underpinned by examples that demonstrate its applicability. The approach provides new insights into the possibilities of web site specification, and it will be made apparent that it serves as a further stepping stone towards better web site models. We believe that this helps in creating better web sites.

1.3 Text structure

The text is structured as follows.

Part One: Introduction

The first part of this text constitutes the introduction and sets the ground for the presentation of the core ideas.

Chapter 1, the current chapter, has introduced into the problem domain and set out the goal for this work.

Chapter 2 summarises the current state of research in the area we are working in. We build upon many sources, and this chapter names them, placing our work into a proper context.

Chapter 3 gives an account on the functional programming language Haskell, which will be used as an example implementation and specification language.

Part Two: Functional Web Site Specifications

The second part introduces the main theme of this work by providing detailed information on a coherent set of specifications for a web site.

Chapter 4 motivates a partition of a web site specification into well-defined parts. Each part focusses on one particular concern. This chapter also introduces an example web site that will be referred to in subsequent chapters.

Chapters 5, 6, 7, 8, 9, and 10 then detail on the respective specification parts: the content model, the query and updating functions, the dynamics functions, the page functions, the navigation structure, and the presentation functions.

Chapter 11 describes the application of the findings to a second example web site, a travel agency system.

Part Three: Conclusion

The third part concludes this work. It comprises two short chapters:

Chapter 12 looks back and provides a summary of this work.

Chapter 13 looks ahead and identifies possible future work.

Appendix

The appendix completes this text.

Chapter 14 contains a brief description of the implementation using the web application server Zope and its integration with Haskell.

Chapter 15 has a glossary of terms. We will use the symbol ◇ in the main text to mark a word as being used as defined in the glossary.

The bibliography will be found there as well.

Typography

This text is typeset using LATEX. I have used this system to the best of my knowledge, which is not very comprehensive, so there will most certainly be plenty of typographical errors and annoyances. Blame me!

After quite some hours of experimentation and reading, I decided in favour of the KOMA book class, in combination with the lmodern package to use the type 1 version of the computer modern fonts. There are nicer fonts, but the computer modern fonts are cheaper (well, 'free' is more accurate), and they look sufficiently nice for English text with not too many capital letters.

The visual experience is greatly improved by the microtype package, which performs almost magical computations to achieve character protrusion into the margin as well as font expansion, significantly improving the greyness of the pages. The tables were set with commands from the booktabs package, so the horizontal lines should look much better compared to the standard ones. All source code fragments are beautifully typeset using the listings package, which saved huge amounts of work because the code can be kept almost 'as-is'.

Kudos to the authors of all these packages!

Related Work

'A dwarf standing on the shoulders of a giant may see farther than a giant himself' – This famous quote by Didacus Stella (after [Ste05]) contains the essence of scientific work: create new knowledge by relying on existing knowledge, and offer that new knowledge for others to use, so to create a documented history of knowledge. The pivotal idea that makes this process work is the will to share results, and the trustworthy handling of inherited knowledge by naming those who one inherits from. Thus, one might proclaim: You dwarf, who hath climbed the giant and now standeth on his shoulders, and discovereth new and promising wisdom in the distance, always remember that this cometh not from your own strength alone!

In this spirit, the following sections provide a thorough look into relevant scientific achievements of the past and of the present. As an introduction, the following section 2.1 presents a backbone structure that is employed in the following to identify the most important concerns of web site modelling. Section 2.2 gives more details concerning this structure. Section 2.3 continues by focussing on web engineering processes, and section 2.4 contains descriptions of five model-driven approaches which were selected as prominent examples for ideas that had a great amount of impact on the research work that followed. Section 2.5 shifts the focus towards achievements from the functional 'world' and presents the relevant scientific findings that have surfaced so far.

2.1 Model-driven Approaches

The development of web sites and web applications, and web engineering in general, heavily relies on *models*◇. Models play an almost pivotal role right from the beginning, when starting to gather the requirements, and even more so during analysis, design, implementation, and evolution. This reliance on models is inherited from classical software engineering. As of today, the complexity of web site development projects clearly demands for the application of sound software engineering techniques, and using models is one of them. At the same time, web engineering projects have specific characteristics, like even shorter development times, utmost flexibility, and agility, as well as aspects not found in traditional software projects, like the need to care for hypertext models.

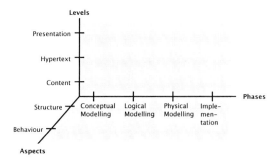

Figure 2.1: Modelling Dimensions ([RS00], p. 2)

The latter aspects will be dealt with near the end of this chapter. First, we will concentrate on giving an overview of current *model-based* web engineering approaches. This overview will be grounded on a set of different aspects of web site modelling. These aspects correspond to a catalogue of common modelling aspects, derived from Wieland Schwinger and Nora Koch's chapter in [KPRR04], and also based on Werner Retschitzegger and Wieland Schwinger's article [RS00], where different modelling methods are compared and a common requirements framework for modelling methods is presented. This framework shows the necessary elements of a modelling method by defining three orthogonal dimensions (cf. figure 2.1):

- Levels – A web site model should reflect a separation of the content level, the hypertext level, and the presentation level. The content level is about the domain of interest and the data used therein. This data is composed into web pages and a navigation structure. This is referred to in the hypertext level. The presentation level, finally, deals with the visual representation – or, in general, the rendering via any appropriate medium – of the elements defined in the hypertext level.

- Aspects – For each level, structural as well as behavioural aspects have to be considered. This means that, e.g., in addition to laying down the data structure at the content level, the dynamics of that data has to be taken into account. The degree of relevance of the behavioural aspect depends on the respective requirements for the concrete web site: some web sites require almost no dynamics at all (e.g., a static web site presenting the documentation of some API), while others put substantial emphasis on dynamics (e.g., an e-commerce web site).

- Phases – The life cycle of a web site can be separated into several phases that serve to emphasise specific elements during the development. Roughly speaking, the phases range from analysis, over design, to implementation. This is not a strict separation of activities, but rather a gradual shift of focus along the timeline of development, and the notion of a *phase* does not say anything about the *process*. See section 2.3 for a discussion on this topic.

There is no consensus on a general sequence of phases and the artefacts needed, but it seems appropriate to state that the models should range from abstract domain representations (conceptual model), technology independent design (logical model) towards technology dependent design (physical model).

In [KPRR04], it is argued to regard *customisation* as an additional dimension, because every element listed above should consider the possibility to adapt itself towards a specific usage context ('circumstances of consumption') [KRS00]. This leads to the notion of a *core* web site that can be transformed into a *customised* web site. *Customisation*◇ is defined to be the 'adaptation of an application's services towards its context' [KPRS03, p. 82]. Context information, and customisation that relies on it, are aspects that gain increasing importance for modern web applications, especially when it comes to *ubiquitous* applications that allow for adaptation and personalisation based on the current visitor's geographical location, the current time of the day and the access device used by the visitor.

One inherent characteristic of a web site is that it changes and evolves over time, and indeed rapidly so. This leads our focus to the high importance of web site *maintenance*. We regard maintenance as being a continuous task, and there is no clear borderline that precisely separates maintenance from 'normal' (pre-maintenance) development. In our terminology, one should speak of a *phase* that has maintenance as its prominent focus. This phase is exceptional to some degree, as it is executed almost permanently. As an example activity, regard configuration management: it is part of maintenance, and it 'happens' all the time.

Every model created during the development of a web site should be critically checked against whether or not it eases maintenance. If the answer is negative, then the model is to be revised. This might sound somewhat drastic, but it is an acknowledged fact that for web sites, maintenance plays an even more important role than it does for traditional software (e.g., [KPRR04, p. 189]). The approaches introduced in the following will therefore have to make their stand against the maintainability requirement.

So far, we have set up a multi-dimensional space that allows for viewing web engineering projects from five different angles. One could quite easily find even more dimensions (e.g., web site quality and its assurance), but we will resist this temptation. Instead, we will subsume additional aspects under the mentioned five and we will discuss these additional aspects whenever the need may arise.

Not every co-ordinate in this five-dimensional space corresponds to a separate model. As was already said, the dimensions are merely views upon a set of integrated models of which each model may cover a number of dimensions or aspects. For the remainder of this text, we want to focus on the artefacts. In [KPRR04], it is suggested to take care of the following topics for a web site project:

- content,

- hypertext,

- presentation, and

- contextuality.

This collection of topics corresponds to the three *levels* listed above, plus the contextuality dimension. For the majority of the projects, each topic will result in (at least) one model. If customisation or any other form of context-awareness is not relevant for a particular project, then the last topic may be omitted altogether.

The following section 2.2 will briefly explain each of these topics. We will give references to other publications in order to show how the modelling problem is seen in current literature, and we will also point out how the respective topic will be treated by our own view on web site specification. After that, section 2.3 will discuss alternatives concerning the development *process*, particularly by comparing light-weight and heavy-weight processes. Finally, a representative selection of five approaches and methods is presented in more detail (section 2.4).

2.2 Modelling Topics

2.2.1 Content

Many, if not most, model-driven web engineering approaches suggest to create a content model based on entities and relationships or on classes and associations. The content model is necessary to have a firm understanding of the information space that forms the core of the web site. The model captures the domain of interest and often also serves as a data schema. It encompasses both the structural as well as the behavioural aspects.

A majority of the current approaches employs the UML for the notation of diagrams. Some approaches rely on proprietary notations for some of the diagram types. However, the application of UML (and its extension mechanisms) seems to be the trend, shown by the fact that most of the recent approaches go into this direction. The main reasons stated for using UML are the availability of tools ([GN02, p. 2]), the fact that the UML is well-documented ([KKH01, p. 2]), and the coherence gained by using UML for a web application that is connected to other systems that are already modelled using UML ([Con99, p. 64]). As of today, one can state that using UML class diagrams for the notation of entity-relationship views simply is standard practice.

The structural aspect covered by the content model is commonly expressed via a class diagram. At this stage, the classes correspond to concepts of the application domain, and the whole object-oriented modelling arsenal (associations, aggregation, generalisation, constraints, patterns and the like) may be employed to build an appropriate abstraction of that particular section of reality. The behavioural aspect may be modelled by state/transition models (statecharts, activity diagrams).

2.2.2 Hypertext

It has already been pointed out that hypertext is one of the specific characteristics of web sites. Hypertext implies non-linearity, an aspect that sets web sites apart from software that is not presented through the web. In the literature reviewed so far, there is no consensus on how this navigational aspect of a web site should be modelled. While this sort of consensus seems to have been reached for the content modelling by concentrating on object-oriented (or comparable) methods, the hypertext modelling is mostly based on new and specific languages and concepts.

At least, there is a common understanding of hypertext as being a collection of *nodes* that are interconnected by *links*. Thus, the hypertext model must comprise a statement on the *types of nodes* used, it must define the actual nodes (i.e., which content is presented on a particular node) and it must define the links between the nodes. In general, it is possible to define *multiple* hypertexts for one web site, which corresponds to having different 'views' on the same amount of data, which can be exploited, for example, to implement personalisation.

In order to provide some more background information, the existing approaches that seem to have gained some amount of importance will be introduced briefly. The comparative study by Nora Koch ([Koc99]) presents the core aspects of eleven 'methodologies for hypermedia and web development' (p. 1) and perspicuously shows differences and similarities. This includes the *methods* used in the respective approaches (process, technique, graphical representation, notation, tools), the *concepts* (terminology) defined, and the *phases* covered. The study relates on the approaches listed in table 2.1.

Avoiding to treat each of these approaches in detail and focussing on the navigational aspects only, the study can be summarised as follows. The first observation is that the approaches are quite hard to compare, because they all have different foci, different terminology, different backgrounds and different goals. Despite this almost discouraging fact, the study succeeds in distilling a common sequence of steps that are to be taken in order to create a hypermedia or a web application. All approaches more or less require to model the navigation structure after designing the domain model and before shifting the focus towards user interface design. The second observation is that navigation relies on views on the conceptual domain model and that the definition of navigable objects (the navigation space) is separate from the definition of the navigation structure itself. There exist some common access structures like indexes, menus, or guided tours, that can be used for defining complex navigation objects. Hypermedia applications, more than web applications, make use of different kinds of links like bidirectional or structural links.

In a nutshell, the problem of defining the navigation model can be divided into two tasks: defining the navigation space, i.e., the set of objects or nodes that can be visited, and defining the navigation structure, i.e., telling *how* these objects can be navigated.

The *navigation space* should be a view on the conceptual model. It is not clear, however, how this view is to be defined. It may not be sufficient to constrain oneself to a one-to-one mapping from domain concepts to navigation classes, as suggested in [KKH01]. Here, a navigation class corresponds to a concept in the domain model, possibly extended by derived attributes that are defined by OCL expressions. In the OO-$\mathcal{H}$Method ([GCP00]), attributes can additionally be given a visibility tag (defining whether the attribute should be always visible, always hidden, or 'referenced,' which means that one further navigation step is necessary to view this attribute) and a list of perspectives that further differentiate the attribute (language, rhetorical style, or presentation medium). More flexibility is

Abbreviation and Name		Authors	Citation
HDM	Hypermedia Design Method	Garzotto, Paolini, and Schwabe	[GPS93]
RMM	Relationship Management Methodology	Isakowitz, Stohr, and Balasubramanian	[ISB95]
EORM	Enhanced Object Relationship Methodology	Lange	[Lan96]
OOHDM	Object-Oriented Hypermedia Design Method	Rossi and Schwabe	[SR95b]
SOHDM	Scenario-based Object-oriented Design Methodology	Lee, Lee, and Yoo	[LLY98]
WSDM	Web Site Design Method	de Troyer and Leune	[DL98]
RNA	Relationship-Navigational Analysis	Bieber, Galnares, and Lu	[BGL98]
—	MacWeb Approach	Nanard and Nanard	[NN95]
HFPM	Hypermedia Flexible Process Modeling	Olsina	
—	OO/Pattern Approach	Thomson, Greer, and Cooke	
—	Lowe-Hall's Engineering Approach	Lowe and Hall	[LH99]

Table 2.1: Web engineering approaches reviewed in [Koc99]

offered in OOHDM ([SR95b]), where the attributes of navigation objects are defined by using SQL-like expressions over the conceptual model. The same procedure is used for links, which are created as views on relationships by giving a source and a target navigation class as well as a logical expression that is evaluated for each navigation object.

When the instance data is available as a graph, appropriate query languages will allow for even more elaborate queries, including complex path expressions and the evaluation of type information. One approach using graph querying is Strudel ([FFLS00]), where the navigation objects are declaratively defined in the StruQL query language. We also will use graphs on the instance level.

The *navigation structure* uses the navigation objects and defines their relationships. One example of structuring them is the 'navigational context' as defined in OOHDM. A navigational context is a set of nodes with an internal navigational structure, an entry point and associated indexes (access structures). The contexts can be used to produce intra-set navigation. That makes it possible, for example, to define a set of navigation objects (all professors teaching software technology courses, say) and creating a sequence in which the objects can be visited (using, e.g., 'next' and 'previous' links). This allows to create links that are not present in the conceptual model in form of relationships, but which make sense during navigational modelling. At the same time, the sets are first-class objects and can be treated just like the other navigation objects. The contexts are put into relation using a context schema.

A different way of modelling the navigation structure is to use statecharts, as proposed, e.g., in [LHYT00] and [GN02]. The states represent screens or pages, and the transitions clearly show what happens when a particular event occurs while the system is in a certain state. The events normally are the result of user interaction (especially the activation of hyperlinks) or may be triggered by the run-time system itself (for example when a scheduled time-out fires). The screens correspond to navigation objects.

On a higher level of abstraction, hypermedia design patterns (cf. [GC00] for a list of patterns) may be used to refer to common problems and their solution. Some modelling approaches provide means to conveniently apply patterns, by including dedicated notations for some of the patterns. One example is the *landmark* pattern. This pattern is used to specify that a certain page (e.g., the home page) should always be directly accessible, which may be achieved by including a corresponding hyperlink in every page of the web site. The Web Modeling Language (WebML), which will be introduced in section 2.4.1, lets the designer use the landmark pattern directly.

2.2.3 Presentation

There is no denying the fact that web sites are experienced by web site visitors primarily via *visual* cues. The presentation of web pages is therefore very important, as it defines the 'look and feel' of the web site. The visitor, who is generally the authoritative source for many requirements that are imposed on the construction of a web site (cf. user-centred design, [Gar03]), must be able to use the site in a convenient way, and the presentation contributes heavily to the usability of the web site.

We cannot and will not delve into the issues that are relevant during the design of a web site in respect to its graphical presentation. It is our intention here to provide an overview on how the presentation can be *defined* in principle, and not how the final presentation should be like. That is, we are interested in the *techniques of defining* the presentation, and not in the respective outcome of these definitions for concrete web sites. The latter is a completely separate concern, and it is common to use dedicated software tools for this task, and to have graphic design specialists take care of creating appropriate solutions. In general, the iterative process of defining the look and feel of a web site involves the production of page mock-ups which are used as (sources for) page templates.

As far as the techniques are concerned, several suggestions exist. In the UWE approach ([KKH01, p. 20], [HK01], see also section 2.4.5), UML diagrams, notably class diagrams with nested composition, are used for the notation of an abstract page layout and 'sketches' of the user interface. Other approaches employ specific notations or languages ([SdAPM99], [FFLS00]). It is also an option to use standard languages like XSLT to create web documents including presentation from XML documents that only contain information about the *abstract* structure of a page.

2.2.4 Contextuality

The consideration of context information to achieve adaptation of web sites is an emerging problem that gains increasing attention. An important concept is that of *ubiquitous* web applications, i.e., applications that include personalisation, localisation, as well as adaptation to the current geographical context of the user and to the device that the pages are delivered to.

The adaptation of a web site is inherently cross-cutting, as it may be applied to almost any part of the system, be it the content model, the hypertext structure, or the presentation, or even the contextuality itself. It is therefore crucial to define precisely to which degree the adaptation shall take place, and what shall be achieved by it. These definitions happen at the time of modelling, which makes it clear that adaptation is different from maintenance. The adaptation of a web site is always laid down in the models, thus, it is anticipated change, and not the reaction to alterations of the requirements or to environmental changes.

The evaluation in [KPRS03] provides a thorough overview on current approaches and how they support adaptation. In particular, the article presents a framework that can be used to classify approaches, and also to identify the different aspects of adaptation. The framework suggests to differentiate between *adaptation* and *context* as two orthogonal dimensions, and to regard *customisation* as the combination of both. The adaptation dimension captures the *kind* of adaptation, i.e., *what* is to be changed, the *subject* of adaptation, and the *process* of adaptation. The context dimension is considered with the 'why and when' of the changes. Using this framework, 10 approaches are classified and compared to one another.

2.3 Web Engineering Processes

The process of developing a web site is in itself subject to scientific research, and current literature provides a number of contributions and suggestions that help in the clarification of the steps necessary to create and maintain a web site. In this context, the term *process* means to focus on the *organisation* of these development steps, in contrast to a *method*, which provides concrete advice on how to proceed on an operational level.

Chapter 10 in [KPRR04] provides an overview of the most important directions of research while comparing light-weight versus heavy-weight approaches. Starting from a catalogue of requirements that should be fulfilled by a decent approach, two prominent representatives, Extreme Programming (XP, [Bec00]) and the Rational Unified Process (RUP, [Kru00]), are assessed. Neither approach satisfies the needs completely.

While XP is in widespread use today, it has to be noted that it lacks proper scalability to very large and complex applications that require big development teams. Since the size and complexity of the applications tends to increase in the foreseeable future, XP might not be the first choice for those kinds of projects. XP is, however, very well suited for current web engineering projects that are classified by short development times, tight budgets, rapid changes to the requirements, and the preference of quick results in favour of elaborate and future-proof solutions.

The RUP, on the other hand, demands too much precision in too early stages of development, which is not realistic for many current web engineering projects. Requirements for web applications change often, and at any time, which makes it very hard to provide a *vision* of the final system as early as in the inception phase.

Chances are good, however, that processes like the RUP gain importance for future web engineering projects. As soon as a greater amount of stability is reached and more experience is available that makes it possible to treat web application development like the development of well-understood products rather than the one-shot production of artefacts with fuzzy and ever changing requirements, elaborate and heavy-weight processes will be applicable and will perform very well. One can clearly see a parallel to the history of traditional software engineering.

2.4 Selected Web Engineering Approaches

This section provides some more detail on selected web engineering approaches, so to underpin the aforementioned general findings using concrete projects. In the following, we will look into WebML, Strudel, OOHDM, RMM, and UWE.

The survey presented by Piero Fraternali (see [Fra99]) also regards additional tools and approaches that are particularly suited for the creation of 'data-intensive web applications.' This also includes approaches that are not inherently model-driven. Our selection is strictly confined to approaches that rely on models.

2.4.1 Web Modeling Language (WebML)

The *Web Modeling Language* (WebML) is a comprehensive language for the description of web applications ([CFB+03]). It features a graphical notation of the hypertext model that allows for the visual definition of the navigation structure and the navigation objects. The model can alternatively be written as an XML document that allows for the inclusion of details not expressible in the visual language. WebML is accompanied by a suggestion for an iterative and incremental development process (see also [MMCF03, p. 3]). The language is also supported by a CASE tool, called WebRatio, that provides a visual environment for editing specification documents and is able to translate the XML representations of the specifications into a complete implementation.

The basis for the web application is formed by the *data model*. It captures the 'conceptual schema' ([CFB+03, p. 61]) that represents the application domain. The data model can be expressed as an extended entity-relationship model (one extension is the introduction of derived attributes specified by OCL expressions) or as an UML class diagram.

The *hypertext model* is regarded as the second part of a conceptual modelling phase that comprises the data design and the hypertext design. The hypertext model defines the logical organisation of data into pages. The key ingredients of these models are pages, units, and links, organized into modularisation constructs called areas and site views.

A *page* is the entity that is actually delivered to a user. It is composed of *units*, which are the atomic building blocks that specify the page's content by referring to the data model. Figure 2.2 depicts a simple example page called Home that consists of two units. A unit can be a *data unit* that shows information about a single object, a *multidata*

Figure 2.2: WebML example page

unit that shows information about a set of objects, an *index unit* that lists consolidated information about a set of objects, a *scroller unit* that allows to browse through a set of objects sequentially, or an *entry unit* that represents a data entry form for the user to fill out. Figure 2.2 shows one scroller unit (left) and an index unit (right), both connected to the same class Artist.

Links connect units and pages, thus establishing the navigation structure. Links can be differentiated into *inter-page* links and *intra-page* links, depending on whether or not they cross a page boundary. A link is called inter-page when it connects two units that reside on different pages, or when it connects two pages directly. A link is an intra-page link when both its origin and destination are on the same page. Links may also transport information, which may be a set of values given by a form entry unit, or an object identifier of a selected entity in an index unit. Information transporting links are called *contextual*, while the others are *non-contextual* links. Apart from being manually activated by the web site visitor, a link may also be declared *automatic* which involves its immediate activation upon page computation. This can be used for links that should transport default values from one unit to another in a situation where no particular value is available, for example because the visitor has not yet selected one. If a link shall not even be visible, it can be marked as being a *transport* link. These links serve to define data flow between units, without resulting in a visible rendering in form of hyperlinks or buttons.

An *area* recursively contains other sub-areas or pages. This allows to define hierarchies of related pages, for example in order to collect all pages that deal with a company's products into one area, and to create a second area that contains pages that implement a discussion forum for the customers. A *site view* is a collection of areas and single pages, so to define multiple hypertext views upon the same set of pages, for example directed towards different identified user groups.

WebML's strength lies in the intuitive graphical notation for the hypertext model that can be used to specify entire web sites. The language is particularly well suited for web sites that are data-driven, that is, web sites whose primary responsibility is to present data that conforms to a data model. By using *operation units*, changes to the data can also be modelled. This involves the creation, modification, or deletion of objects.

One other benefit is the support for high-level navigation patterns. Using a scroller unit, for example, it is straightforward to create a guided tour over a set of objects. In the general case, however, when the guided tour should comprise of an arbitrary set of

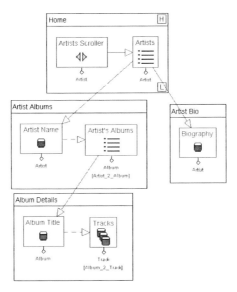

Figure 2.3: WebML example web site

Figure 2.4: WebML example web site data model

pages, the pages have to be connected by links manually. Nevertheless, many navigation patterns can be put in place by creating and connecting only a few units. See [CFB⁺03, sec. 3.7] for a compilation of nine patterns. Yet some other patterns are built right into the language, like the landmark pattern, which is modelled by attaching a corresponding symbol (the capital letter 'L') to a page that should be accessible from all other pages in the same area. The generation process then takes care to create the necessary hyperlinks in the affected pages.

Figure 2.3 shows a complete example web site, consisting of four pages. The underlying data model is depicted in figure 2.4.

The WebML, and the whole approach that goes along with it, is comprehensive, consistent, and powerful. Due to the availability of tools that support it, web sites can be constructed with little effort. The underlying models guarantee the web site's consistency and easy maintainability; and also its portability, because the actual implementation platform is not prescribed in advance.

The most outstanding feature of this approach is the visual language for the notation of the composition of a web site from pages and page fragments. It allows to construct pages by combining the provided types of units, which in turn can be related to concepts from the data model. The navigation structure is made explicit by inserting links between units and/or pages. All this contributes to the ease of use, and shows that the visual language is well designed.

The expressiveness of the language is confined, however. Therefore, facts not expressible with the visual language can be written in an XML notation, which is the actual representation that is used throughout the system. The visual language is an add-on, and it is the corresponding XML document that represents the authoritative source. For many applications, the visual language is sufficiently expressive, and direct modifications or extensions of the XML documents are necessary only in very rare cases.

In principle, the XML documents are not capable of expressing non-regular page structures, so that the composition of the pages cannot be arbitrary. This limitation should not only scarcely surface in practice, and might be of theoretical relevance only. Note that our approach, which will employ a functional programming language to specify the page structure, enables the full range of flexibility at this point.

2.4.2 Strudel

The Strudel approach ([FFLS00, FST99]) employs graph technology in combination with functions in order to specify web sites, making it a very interesting subject of study. The initial work on this approach was conducted at AT&T in the late 1990ies.

Introduction to Strudel

The Strudel way to modelling a web site is to write a query in the Strudel query language, StruQL. Not only does this query define which external data is to be included in the web site, but also – and more importantly so – it defines the *structure* of the web site. The query produces the *site graph* by specifying how vertices and edges are to be constructed. The site graph represents the whole web site in form of content *and* structure. As a special feature, the site graph can be taken as input for another StruQL query that produces a new site graph based on data available in the first site graph. Consequently, StruQL is called a compositional query language.

A StruQL query is a declarative specification of a web site. Nodes in the graph can be declared as being pages or page components. The actual creation of HTML code is performed by applying a *template language* to the site graph. The site author can attach one template to each node. Using these templates, HTML code (or whatever language is chosen as the output language) is computed for each node in the site graph. Depending on whether a node is a page or a page component, a whole page or just an HTML fragment is generated, respectively.

Edges in the site graph are labelled connections between two nodes. They can be used in path expressions to navigate between nodes.

The template language uses an HTML-like syntax to intersperse control flow statements (iteration, alternative, expression evaluation, form and form field generation) into the text that is left unchanged. For example,

```
<html>
<title>Hello World! Example</title>
<h1>Hello World! Example</h1>

<SFOR h IN Hello ORDER=ascend KEY=name>
  <SFMT @h EMBED><br>
</SFOR>
</html>
```

produces a complete HTML page with a list of formatted objects contained in a collection named Hello. For each object – the objects are nodes in the site graph – the HTML code attached to that particular node is included in succession.

Functions in StruQL Queries

A StruQL query can contain function declarations and function calls. A function produces a graph and returns a reference to its root node. Thus, a function call is like a node constructor. The function body consists of a StruQL query describing the sub-graph.

The sub-graph generated by a function is disjoint from the graph constructed by the rest of the query and is connected to the rest only by edges to its root.

Functions can be evaluated eagerly or lazily. The appropriate strategy can be chosen by the user by adorning the function call with a corresponding prefix ('&' or '@', respectively). The semantics of both strategies are, disregarding the termination property, equivalent, i.e., both return the same result if both functions terminate.

Form Pages

A *form* in Strudel may only occur on an edge between nodes. When traversing this edge, the form variable's values are requested from the user and passed on to a lazily evaluated function on the destination node.

'Conceptually, a query with forms defines an infinite graph, because the form's range of values can be infinite.' [FFLS00, section 4.1]. As with any lazily evaluated function, the site graph contains a *closure* node that conveys information necessary to evaluate the function.

The definition of a form itself (i.e., the fields it consists of) is attached to the origin node as a corresponding template. The HTML generator can check that all required variables are bound in the form definition. The generated HTML pages are built in a way to submit the form data to a CGI script that eventually calls the StruQL query interpreter (a command-line script) and instructs it to evaluate the function defined on the destination node. The actual values from the form fields are passed along as parameters.

The Strudel system treats forms as dynamic pages that are not materialised until requested. Apart from that, forms do not differ from any other page, in that they, too, are created by evaluating a query, constructing the site graph, and returning the HTML code that is produced by the HTML generator for the given node in the graph.

Virtual Pages

Strudel also supports what we will call *virtual pages*, i.e., pages whose identity is not pre-defined, but is rather calculated by means of a parameter (cf. section 8.2.4). This allows for having an arbitrary large set of pages with the same structure but different identifiers. This construction is necessary, for example, when one wants to specify that there shall exist an identifiable page for every object in a given set, but the set itself is not known until run-time.

StruQL offers two concepts that are interesting for this task: *collections* and *skolem functions*.

Collections are named sets of nodes. Membership tests (i.e., tests of the form 'Is node n contained in collection c?') can be used in predicates. A query may contain so-called collect clauses that put nodes into collections. Using collections, pages can be grouped together and actions can be defined on a whole set of pages (for example, create a link from each page in a set to another page).

Skolem functions are used to create new nodes. A nullary skolem term defines a unique node. When parameters are supplied, a skolem function always maps to the same node for the same list of parameter values. If, for example, the variable a can be bound to a member in a set A, then the term $HomePage(a)$ identifies exactly one node for each possible value of a. This way, sets of nodes can be constructed (and identified) based on data originating from an external source. When a skolem term is evaluated and the specified node does not yet exist, it is created. Otherwise, a reference to the existing node is returned.

Skolem terms directly correspond to virtual pages, with the difference that skolem terms can comprise any number of arguments that define the mapping to a concrete page object, whereas the identifier of a virtual page is defined by one argument alone.

A collection is a concept not directly mappable to a world where every page is a function, as we will suggest to do. A collection would allow to group functions together based on their name. However, collections in StruQL should be regarded as a feature of the query language, allowing to attach 'tags' to nodes. From this point of view, a collection is just a special form of extending nodes with an additional attribute (one can imagine each node having the attribute isMemberIn with the type 'list of String') and using this attribute in expressions.

2.4.3 Object-Oriented Hypermedia Design Model (OOHDM)

Following the process suggested along the Object-Oriented Hypermedia Design Model (OOHDM), four different activities are to be carried out: conceptual design, navigational design, abstract interface design, and implementation ([RSL99]). It is considered very important to separate conceptual from navigational design since they deal with different aspects. In fact, the conceptual design should not be tailored towards a Web application, but should be the same as for any other 'legacy' application. The Web environment is not considered until during navigational design.

Relationships in the conceptual model can be directly used in the navigational model, as there is a standard one-to-one mapping from a relationship to a link. Additional classes can be introduced that define views on the conceptual model. Other kinds of classes define access structures such as query interfaces, browsers, or choosers ([SR95a]). [RSL99] stresses explicitly that the objects a user navigates are *not* the conceptual objects and thus have to be treated differently. It is also important that the navigational design is typically user dependant, i.e., there will be different navigational designs for each group of site visitors.

The navigational model usually contains link classes that represent relationships from the conceptual model. The source concept and the target concept are provided as attributes. As such, a link class can be regarded as a view on a conceptual relationship.

Defining views on the conceptual model by creating corresponding navigational classes follows the observer pattern. Navigational objects can get notified when content changes, and they can request functionality from conceptual classes (like, for example, changing persistent data). A simple query language is used to describe navigational objects (nodes).

OOHDM introduces the notion of *navigational contexts*. A navigational context is a set of navigational objects with an own navigational structure. A navigational object can appear in multiple contexts (sets). The motivation for navigational contexts derives from the observation that a node must be treated differently according to the context it appears in. For example, following a 'next' link from a node representing a book by Shakespeare might lead to a second Shakespeare book when the context is 'books by Shakespeare,' but it might lead to something completely different when the context is 'English books'.

After defining the navigational design, it must be specified how to present the navigational classes to the users. This is achieved during abstract interface design, where perceptible objects are introduced that map to corresponding navigational objects.

Schwabe et al. also work on *navigational patterns* that describe recurring problems and their solutions. For example, the landmark pattern denotes that a point in navigational space should be visible from all other nodes in the system. In a web application, this implies generating a link to the landmark from every page. This simplifies the navigational schema, because the links do not have to considered explicitly. Also, it should be noted that a landmark is not occuring in the conceptual model, but that it is a navigational artefact. The idea of using patterns found its way into many approaches, as was already seen for the WebML (see section 2.4.1).

2.4.4 Relationship Management Methodology (RMM)

Modelling an hypermedia application with the Relationship Management Methodology (RMM) involves creating an entity-relationship (ER) model of the application domain. After that, so-called *slice diagrams* can be created which show how to present a single, complex entity on separate pages. Each slice groups one or more attributes of an entity, and there will be one page per slice. The creation of slice diagrams is optional.

The navigational design of the hypermedia application starts with a decision about which relationships of the ER model should be made accessible for navigation. The navigation is modelled explicitly using a visual language with specific *access primitives*. These are

- Unidirectional Link: The visitor can travel from page A to page B.

- Bidirectional Link: The visitor can travel back and forth between pages A and B.

- Index: The visitor can choose from a table of contents listing entity instances.

- Guided Tour: The visitor is led through a sequence of pages. Each page is linked to its successor (and optionally to its predecessor and back to the start of the tour). A guided tour can be *circular* (last page links back to first one) or *with return to main* (last page links to an overview page).

- Grouping: The visitor can choose from a menu-like structure showing an overview of certain pages. This is a special kind of index.

Each access primitive has an own graphical notation (symbol type). These are integrated into an entity-relationship diagram in place of relationships. The resulting model is called RMDM (Relationship Management Data Model).

2.4.5 The UML-based Web Engineering Approach (UWE)

The UML-based Web Engineering Approach (UWE) by Koch/Kraus/Hennicker employs UML diagrams to capture the results of modelling the different aspects of a web application, starting with a use case model to capture the requirements. The use case model serves as a basis for a conceptual model (class diagram). This is then used to model the navigation, resulting in two kinds of models:

- the navigation space (*which* objects can be visited), and

- the navigation structure (*how* are the objects accessed).

The two models are notated as UML class diagrams with special stereotypes.

The *navigation space* defines 'views' on the conceptual model. The modeller can decide which classes from the conceptual model appear in the navigation space model. Attributes from classes of the conceptual model can be omitted and additional (derived) attributes can be added for each navigation space class (node). The associations from the conceptual model are normally kept in the navigation space model, and additional associations are included as 'short-cuts.' At will, OCL restrictions can be attached.

The *navigation structure* model describes how a relation between two navigation space classes (nodes) is to be made accessible for the visitor. As in the RMM, several access primitives (index, guided tour, query, and menu) can be used to define how each of the relations should be transformed. In the process, these relations are replaced by 'intermediate' classes (using one of the four stereotypes index, guided tour, query, and menu).

A query class can be used to model an OCL select operation. The query string is stored in an attribute. Each query can be connected to an index (resulting in the query result being presented in form of a list, allowing the visitor to pick the desired object) or to a guided tour (the objects returned by the query are presented as a guided tour).

The UWE approach continues with defining the presentation. The authors suggest drawing sketches of the abstract user interface and using them for storyboarding. Storyboard scenarios are 'sequences of user interface views in the order in which the user can navigate from one view to another.' The interface sketches are built of presentation classes and additional items like anchors, forms, images, etc.

The suggested approach is supported by a CASE tool, ArgoUWE.

2.5 Functional Approaches

This section introduces related work in the area of functional programming that is of relevance for the ideas presented in this text. It is not our intention – and it would not make much sense – to come up with a profound introduction into functional programming. Even confining ourselves to the most important aspects would result in a vast amount of approaches, techniques, and ideas, that had to be considered. Thus, although it is a daunting task to make a minuscule selection from such a rich set of valuable scientific research, we will present a very limited view upon this field, only comprising of the work that has direct connections to what is offered here.

We will use Haskell as an example language for the functional specifications. For a basic introduction to this language and to existing tools and libraries that we will employ, the reader is referred to chapter 3. The current section will concentrate on related work that is of a more general nature and which is directly linked to the modelling aspects just described in section 2.1.

The presentation of the related work is structured by the respective approaches' focus. First, we shall consider those whose focus lies on *producing* web sites or single web pages and making them available to the web site visitor. This comprises techniques to generating web pages, running dynamic and interactive web sites, and doing the actual HTTP serving. Second, we present selected approaches that address the particular sub-problem of specifying and performing data integration into generated web pages.

2.5.1 Web Site Generation

The following approaches deal with the generation of whole web sites or single pages.

Generating Web Pages

There are a number of libraries for generating HTML and XML documents. For an extensive list, see [Ben05] and the library section on [PC04]. Examples are HaXML ([WR05]), the Haskell XML Toolbox ([Sch02], [Sch05]), WASH/HTML ([Thi02], see also below), and LAML ([Nør05]), just to name a view.

Of particular interest are approaches that employ any kind of type checking in order to guarantee that generated XML documents are well-formed (i.e., syntactically correct) and valid (i.e., comply to a given document type definition (DTD) or XML Schema). One basic idea is to provide a *domain specific embedded language* (DSEL). This is a very general concept, whose application is not confined to functional languages; the idea shall be presented briefly: The languages are called *embedded* because they are defined in terms of a host language, like, e.g., Haskell. A DSEL defines a domain specific vocabulary in form of a set of data types and functions that can be used to construct DSEL terms. The host language is used to actually write down these terms, which, in addition, permits to make use of the features provided by the host language, like, e.g., its type system or built-in functions. In general, it is avoided to demand syntactical or semantical extensions to the host language itself.

The greater number of these document-producing approaches focusses on the generation of documents in *one* particular language. This may be (X)HTML, or, in the general case, any XML language that is defined by a given DTD. However, the point is that the terms one writes are specifically mirroring the chosen output language, i.e., they are not abstract. If one wishes to describe documents that are not targeted towards a specific output medium, one has to resort to approaches that support arbitrary XML languages (those that only support (X)HTML won't do), define an abstract language, code the terms using this language, and perform a post-processing step on the generated output or on the term structure.

An example of a DSEL approach to implementing XML-generating functional programs is presented in [Thi02] by Peter Thiemann. His approach is called *WASH/HTML*, and is also a part of WASH (Web Authoring System Haskell) that helps in the construction and execution of interactive web sites (see below for a description of that system). In WASH/HTML, the constraints posed on an XML document by a DTD are modelled by corresponding Haskell types, consisting of multi-parameter type classes and accompanying instance declarations. The necessary Haskell code is synthesised from a given DTD.

Combinator functions are provided that actually build the terms. The functions are declared in a form that allows an '*element-transforming style*' of programming ([Thi02, p. 4]), which results in uncluttered Haskell code that closely mirrors the XML structure and that also avoids subtle typing problems which occur with child elements of different types that have to be stored in one sequence. The general idea is to represent XML elements by functions rather than values, and to express the composition of elements by functions as well.

The approach does not enforce full validity of the documents, however, but 'quasi validity' ([Thi05a, p. 9]). Ordering constraints on child elements are not checked, because constraints like these cannot be conveniently modelled by the Haskell type system without employing language extensions or resulting in less attractive code for the actual term construction. While it is easy to check a given document for full validity, it is hard to guarantee that a program never produces a non-valid document.

One other aspect of Thiemann's approach not yet mentioned is the support for templating. Documents can be assembled from fragments by using a template (master) document that is *parameterised*. Thus, document parts can be inserted into the master document at places defined in the master itself. It is worth noting that the *types* of the parameters (i.e., of the fragments to be inserted) are well taken into account. This means that one cannot put an element into a place where this element is disallowed by the DTD. Doing so results in a compile-time error.

Halipeto ([Coo05]) is a simple template system that can be used to produce small, static web sites. Templates are XHTML documents with special mixed-in XML elements and attributes. The additional elements and attributes are designated with a namespace identifier. Halipeto parses the documents and triggers Haskell functions for each of the registered extensions. The result of a call is then inserted into the original docment. The functions receive as parameter a *context* that enables them to access the document structure of the document they are called upon, the site structure, and a simple, text-based database. Quite a few functions are already predefined, including database accessing functions, iterators, and condition-checkers. The user is free to add custom functions at will.

Running Dynamic Web Sites

WASH/CGI by Peter Thiemann ([Thi05a], [Thi05b]) is an elaborate approach to writing interactive web applications in Haskell. To this purpose, a DSEL is provided, consisting of four sub-languages, where each tackles one specific aspect:

documents
 The document sub-language is used to create XHTML documents. The language is the already introduced WASH/HTML (see above).

sessions

The session sub-language is used to write interactive scripts without having to explicitly deal with the constraints imposed by the statelessness of HTTP. The language includes functions that wrap interaction steps and take care of sending output to the client and of properly resuming the application after the client's answer is received.

widgets

The so-called widget sub-language is used to handle forms and the passing of values between the client and the server. This includes type conversions from bare strings, as dictated by HTTP, into proper Haskell types. If a conversion fails, e.g., due to incorrect input by the client, error messages are automatically sent back to the client. The server program is not continued until all requested values are received and properly converted.

persistence

The persistence sub-language is used to store data that can be shared among sessions as well as data that only belongs to one particular client interaction.

All four languages are integrated and they can be combined freely.

The approach provides a set of functions that lets the web site designer 'program' the entire web site in Haskell, in a comparably convenient way. The focus clearly lies on highly *interactive* web sites (i.e., web applications) that involve sequences of interactions between a client and the server. The idea is to write down the code for those web applications ignoring the fact that, between each interaction step, complex communication is necessary between the client and the server. The server must generate forms and send them to the client, the user fills the forms and sends them back to the server, values must be validated and converted, and, being the hardest part, the interaction must continue at the point were it was last left. Rather than exposing all this to the developer, the abstractions provided by the respective sub-languages make the application look like a traditional, GUI-based application.

The abstraction from an interactive, sequential program is achieved by founding on *log replaying* and *call-back functions*. Whenever the server program sends a message to the client and has to wait for it to answer, the server program stops. It is only the arrival of the client's answer that restarts the program and resumes the interaction at the correct point. In order for this to work, the server program ensures that every interaction is *logged* and correspondingly *replayed* upon restart, so that the last available state is rebuilt and the program can continue as if no interruption had occurred at all. The logging includes both the output of and the input to the respective single interaction steps. As each step is a function that is required to yield the same output for the same input, and all outputs are recorded in the log, the state that prevailed when the server sent its last request to the client can be reconstructed by returning the stored results for each necessary function call.

The interconnection between two interaction steps is defined via call-back functions, which are passed as parameters to those functions that compose a page. If, during log replay, the activation of an interactive element is encountered, e.g., a submit button, the specified call-back function is executed and the result of this function is taken as the next output in the chain of interaction.

<bigwig> ([BMS02]) is a high-level, imperative, extensible, domain-specific language for the implementation of interactive web sites. The language was developed systematically by evaluating the requirements of current web engineering projects. The project team found that the pivotal aspects were sessions, concurrency control, dynamic documents, form field validation, integration with databases, and security. The language was designed to handle these aspects coherently and on an accurate abstraction level. Programs written in the <bigwig> language are compiled rather than interpreted. The compiler output comprises HTML files, CGI programs compiled for the target web server machine, JavaScript files, and Java applets, and the web site thus produced should run on almost any common web server.

In contrast to a DSEL, which is *embedded* in an existing language, the approach taken in the <bigwig> project was to develop a *new* and distinct language. This language unquestionably fulfils all requirements identified by the project team, and lets the web developer program the web site in a convenient way. The solutions to the aforementioned aspects are comparable to those found for the WASH/CGI approach, if one steps back and regards the two approaches on a very high and strictly conceptual level. It it interesting to see, however, how the solutions are put into practice according to quite different assumptions, namely integrating a language in to an existing, functional, one, versus developing an all-new system and an an imperative language.

The <bigwig> project is discontinued in favour of its successor, JWIG ([MC05]), which is based on Java.

Web Servers

Instead of integrating a Haskell environment into an existing web server, one can as well write the entire web server in Haskell. A report on a successful endeavour of this kind is presented in [Mar02], where an implementation in Concurrent Haskell ([JGF96]) is described that can take it up with systems like Apache for all but the most heavily loaded web sites. The web server developed by Simon Marlow was used by Martin Sjögren to implement an enhanced version that can be extended with additional plug-ins ([Sjö02]).

A framework for developing HTTP servers is also provided by the *HAppS* project (see [Jac05]).

2.5.2 Data Integration

The models that will be created for the specification of a web site form abstractions from the actual content level data, and the actual technique to access that data is not prescribed. This enables us to use whatever technique seems appropriate for the web engineering project in question. There must, of course, be a well-defined *interface* for the specification to rely upon. With such an interface in place, everything 'below' can be silently exchanged at any time. Eventually, however, the question of the actual implementation has to be answered, and this is where one of the following approaches might come into play.

HaskellDB ([LM99], extended version in [Lei03, chapter 5]) is an approach to provide a type-safe and declarative way to access a *relational database*. The approach is called *domain specific embedded compiler* (DSEC) because it defines a domain specific embedded language (DSEL) inside of Haskell, which is itself a *programming language*, and the Haskell compiler is used to translate the embedded programs into an executable form. HaskellDB defines a number of combinator functions that are used to construct terms that express queries. The terms are automatically transformed into SQL, and the SQL programs can then be executed by a back-end database server.

The advantage of the approach is threefold: firstly, the queries sent to the database system are guaranteed to by syntactically correct; secondly, their semantic correctness is at least enforced insofar as typing errors and misspelled field names are detected at compile time; and thirdly, the approach abstracts from the actual database system, thus providing a high-level interface to any kind of system that speaks SQL. The last point also implies that the programmer wanting to query a database does not have to use SQL directly. This reduces complexity because it avoids having to think and program in two different worlds.

Instead of constructing SQL commands via string operations and sending the commands to the database system, as is common style in many script-based approaches, the combinator functions are used to construct terms that adhere to an abstract syntax. The syntax is based on *relational algebra* and consists of expressions, constant relations, projection (π), renaming (ρ), restriction (σ), union ($\cup$), difference ($-$), and (cartesian) product ($\times$). Note that join ($\bowtie$) is not included because it can be expressed in terms of product, renaming, and restriction. A query is expressed as a term that forms an abstract syntax tree, with the syntax given by an abstract data type that directly reflects the syntactical elements of a relational algebra term. This defines an 'intermediate language'. Terms (i.e., abstract syntax trees) are transformed into SQL commands automatically. This also involves optimisation steps that can be performed *on the term structure*, prior to generating SQL.

Type information for terms in the intermediate language is attached to them by using *phantom types*. Since this is a common technique, phantom types shall be introduced briefly at this point. We rely on the reader having quite some familiarity with Haskell to be able to comprehend the code examples provided below. It might thus be advisable to skip this part at the first time of reading and to have a look at chapter 3 first.

The idea is to have a polymorphic type over a type variable a, where a does not appear in the type expression on the right-hand side of the declaration. The type a is not forgotten, however. The type information is carried along, and the Haskell type checker uses it to preserve type consistency. As an example, consider simple expressions defined by

```
data SimpleExpr
  = BinaryExpr BinaryOperator SimpleExpr SimpleExpr
```

| Constant **String**

If we introduce a wrapping polymorphic type

data Expr a = Expr SimpleExpr

we can enforce constraints in declarations like

(.&&.) :: Expr **Bool** → Expr **Bool** → Expr **Bool**

which defines a combinator function that constructs terms that represent a boolean operator (here: the logical AND). The signature states that it can only be applied to expressions that are of type Expr **Bool**, i.e., expressions that carry a 'label' saying 'this is an expression based on the type **Bool**'. The resulting expression returned by the .&&. function is also of the type Expr **Bool**.

Constant terms are built by using

```
constant :: Show a ⇒ a → Expr a
constant c = Expr (Constant (show c))
```

Functions like these actually stick a type label to an expression. In the case of constant, a value of any basic Haskell type a is transformed into a constant expression of that same type, i.e., Expr a. The value itself is represented as a string, as demanded by the Constant constructor.

The Haskell compiler complains if it encountered an expression like

(constant 4) .&&. (constant **True**)   *-- ill-typed*

because the type of the expression constant 4 is Expr **Int** and thus cannot be used on the first parameter position for .&&. (viz., on the left-hand side) where a value of the type Expr **Bool** is required instead. This prevents such ill-typed expressions from being constructed at all, and errors like that are spotted *at compile time*.

∎

The same principle of phantom types is employed to attach type information to fields (attributes) and relations. For this to work, the schema information from the database has to be available as corresponding Haskell types. The implementation of HaskelDB ([Lei05]) contains a Haskell program called DB/Direct that performs a transformation step by extracting the database schema automatically and generating appropriate Haskell code that contains the type definitions. The current implementation ([AAB+05]) also no longer relies on a Hugs-specific Haskell extension (see [BHA+04]) that had been necessary in the original version, so it can now also be used with GHC.

Haskell

In this text, the functional programming language Haskell is being used for implementation and prototyping as well as for parts of the modelling. As we shall see, the resulting definitions are inherently concise and easy to understand. This chapter introduces the core features of the Haskell language that are relevant for our work. In order to keep this introduction as brief and as concise as possible, we will only regard those features that are specific to Haskell and we will assume that the reader already has *some* familiarity with functional programming languages in general.

According to 'the' Haskell web site [PC04], Haskell is 'a purely functional language[1] featuring static typing, higher-order functions, polymorphism, type classes and monadic effects.' Besides the fact that Haskell is a *functional* programming language, strong emphasis is placed on the *type-fulness*[2] of Haskell. Every Haskell program can be type-checked at compile-time because of the static type system used by the language.

Before turning our focus towards the details of functions and types, however, the language itself shall be introduced briefly. First, in terms of its history, and then with the help of small code examples.

3.1 A Short Introduction to Haskell

3.1.1 A Little Glimpse at the History

The functional programming language Haskell is named after the logician Haskell Brooks Curry (1900–1982), one of the pioneers of the lambda calculus. The language was born in 1987 as the result of the work carried out by a committee who had given itself the task to weave together the current state of the art in the area of functional programming. It was agreed upon designing a common language that fulfilled the following goals (quoted from [JH98]):

---

[1] Capitalisation changed by the author
[2] Coined by Luca Cardelli

- 'It should be suitable for teaching, research, and applications, including building large systems.

- It should be completely described via the publication of a formal syntax and semantics.

- It should be freely available. Anyone should be permitted to implement the language and distribute it to whomever they please.

- It should be based on ideas that enjoy a wide consensus.

- It should reduce unnecessary diversity in functional programming languages.'

After subsequent additions and alterations to the initial proposals, the committee concluded its work by publishing 'The Haskell 98 Language and Library Reports' in early 1999. Since then, many implementations of Haskell appeared that go well beyond the definitions laid down in the report. Yet, Haskell 98 ([JH98]) is still the matter of reference that is adhered to by all of them. It is 'the' stable definition of the language and the libraries that go with it.

As of today, the interpreter Hugs ([OGI04]) and the compiler GHC ([Mar05]) are in widespread use, due to their free availability and good portability.

3.1.2 Code Examples

The syntax and semantics of the Haskell language shall be introduced only informally in this text. The reader is encouraged to refer to the official Haskell 98 report ([JH98]) as the definitive (and formal) source. Moreover, this chapter does not aim at explaining the language in its entirety; rather, we will focus on only those language elements that are deemed necessary to understand the remainder of the text. Apart from the Haskell 98 report, the reader might also benefit from the web page [vI05], providing a very brief but complete, example-based, overview on the Haskell syntax.

In this section, we will help the reader getting a grip on the language by jumping right into it, starting with simple code examples. Whenever a new concept is encountered, it will be explained on the spot, with the help of the current example.

The first example shows a simple function definition[3]:

```
lengthOfList :: [a] → Integer
lengthOfList [] = 0
lengthOfList (x:xs) = 1 + lengthOfList xs
```

---

[3] A note on the typesetting style: All Haskell code is typeset in a 'prettyfied' way, with keywords and predefined identifiers in bold face. Some symbols, like the right arrow $\rightarrow$ or the lambda in λx have different appearance in normal ASCII (one writes `->` and `\x`, respectively), but they look nicer when typeset in the way used in here.

Here, the function lengthOfList is defined. The first line states that it has the type [a] → **Integer**, which is to be read as 'a function mapping a list to an integer'. The first part of this *type expression*, [a], stands for 'any list': brackets denote lists (which are always homogeneous), and the letter a is a type variable that represents any type. The arrow operator → denotes functions. The type **Integer** is predefined in Haskell and represents all possible integer values. The :: operator attaches a type expression (right-hand side) to an expression (left-hand side); it can be read as 'has type'.

The next two lines actually declare the lengthOfList function. This is achieved by the means of *pattern matching*. Each line (equation) contributes to the declaration of the function by stating which values in the domain of the function shall be mapped to which expression. The domain values are given as patterns. The pattern [], for example, matches the empty list. The value of lengthOfList is said to be 0 in this case. The last line contains the pattern (x:xs) which matches any non-empty list with head x and tail xs. Both variables are bound to the matching values (the head and the tail, respectively), and thus can be used in the expression on the right-hand side of the equation. In our example, this is 1 + lengthOfList xs which evaluates to one plus the length of the tail xs. The expression lengthOfList xs is a recursive *function call* of the lengthOfList function with the parameter xs. Note that one can read xs like the plural of x, and it is common to name the tail of a list in this way.

Pattern matching is performed in the order stated by the source code. The evaluation stops at the first match and the corresponding expression is taken as the result. If no pattern matches, a run-time error occurs and the program stops.

When looking at the definition a second time, one will realise that it bears strong resemblance to the familiar mathematical notation

$$lengthOfList(l) = \begin{cases} 0 & , l = [] \\ 1 + lengthOfList(xs) & , l = x : xs \end{cases}$$

when [] denotes the empty list and $x : xs$ the list with head x and tail xs. Thus, it should have become clear that the function lengthOfList recursively calculates the length of a given list by, figuratively speaking, subsequently 'chopping off' one element after the other and counting how many chops can be made before the list is completely taken apart.

The second example (taken from [HPF99]) also offers a function definition. This time, we will declare the function quicksort, which works exactly like the well-known sorting algorithm of the same name ([Hoa62]):

```
quicksort :: Ord a ⇒ [a] → [a]
quicksort [] = []
quicksort (x:xs) = quicksort [y | y ← xs, y<x ] ++ [x] ++ quicksort [y | y ← xs, y≥x]
```

The first line introduces a so-called *context*: The expression **Ord** a states that the type variable a in the following type expression stands for a type that belongs to the *class* **Ord**, which is a predefined *type class* (or just *class* for short) that guarantees that the comparison functions < and ≥ are defined for the given type a. More details on type classes will be provided in section 3.2.2.

The algorithm works as follows: Sorting an empty list results in the empty list, which is what the first equation says. The second equation takes care of the non-trivial case: sorting a non-empty list (x:xs), with the head element x and the remaining list being xs, is achieved by recursively sorting all elements of xs that are smaller than x, appending x to the result of that, and finally concatenating to it the result of sorting all elements of xs that are greater or equal to x. Thus, the first list element is always taken as the pivot element, and the recursive calls sort the two partitions so defined, and concatenating the results yields the fully sorted list.

The elegance and conciseness of the Haskell code clearly is to be attributed to the list comprehension notation that in this case allows us to easily create the two partitions by simply 'writing down' their declarative definitions. The expression [y | y ← xs, y<x] denotes a list of ys that are drawn from the list xs, one after the other, provided that a y satisfies the expression y<x; that is, the resulting list contains all numbers from xs that are smaller than x, the pivot element.

The operator ++ simply concatenates two lists. The expression [x] denotes the list that only contains x. Since function application takes precedence over every infix operator, there is no need to put parentheses around the recursive function calls to quicksort. The second function call contains another list comprehension that works analogous to the first in that it produces a list of all elements from the list xs that are greater or equal to the pivot element.

The first list comprehension could also have been written as **filter** (λy → y<x) xs which generates a new list by applying the boolean expression y<x to every element in the list xs and keeping only those elements y that are smaller than x. The expression λy → y<x is a *lambda abstraction*, i.e., an anonymous function. It takes one parameter y and evaluates to a boolean value defined by the expression y<x.

Note that the list comprehension notation is even more powerful, because arbitrary expressions are allowed in the construction part of the list (before the vertical bar). Thus, one can write [y∗y | y ← xs, y<x] to build a list of squares of the elements y in xs that satisfy y<x. Thus, when used in this form, list comprehension can be regarded as a combination of the application of **map** and **filter**. For a full description of the possibilities of the list comprehension notation, including the application of multiple generators, see [JH98, §3.11].

The functions **map** and **filter** are predefined in the Haskell *Prelude*, which is a collection of definitions that are available in every Haskell implementation. The functions are defined as follows:

```
map :: (a → b) → [a] → [b]
map f [] = []
map f (x:xs) = f x : map f xs

filter :: (a → Bool) → [a] → [a]
filter p [] = []
```

```
filter p (x:xs)
  | p x = x : filter p xs
  | otherwise = filter p xs
```

These declarations shall be discussed one after the other; we will concentrate on **map** first. The signature of the function demonstrates two important concepts of Haskell not yet encountered: higher-order functions and multiple parameters. The function **map** is a higher-order function because its first parameter is a function, and it consumes more than one parameter (two, in this case): One of type (a → b) and one of type [a]. However, one can also say that the type expression (a → b) → [a] → [b] denotes a function type which maps functions from a to b (this is the first parameter of **map**) to a function that maps lists of as to lists of bs. Here, it is essential to know that → associates to the *right*, i.e., the type expression is evaluated as ((a → b) → ([a] → [b])). This means that calling **map** with one parameter, which may be any function that maps as to bs, yields a *function* that may be called with a parameter of the type 'list of as' and that evaluates to an expression of type 'list of bs.'

It is equivalent to think of **map** having two parameters, one function and one list, resulting in a list. This is indeed how the two equations declare the **map** function itself. The first equation in the second line states that applying **map** to a function f and the empty list should result in the empty list. The last line states that applying **map** to a function f and the non-empty list with head x and tail xs should result in a new list (constructed by the colon) with head f x (the result of calling f on x) and the tail **map** f xs, i.e., the list that results when recursively calling **map** with the same f and the remainder of the list xs.

The idea of regarding every function as having only *one* parameter is a central concept called *currying*[4]. Consider the following two function definitions:

```
double :: Integer → Integer
double x = 2 * x

doubleAll :: [Integer] → [Integer]
doubleAll = map double
```

The first function, double, doubles its argument. The second function, doubleAll, doubles all elements in a list of integers by employing the **map** function to do the actual work. The expression **map** double *is* the function that doubles all numbers in a list because **map** is equipped with the function double as its argument, and **map** is declared to return the function that applies this function to every element in a list. The expression **map** double suggests (and rightfully so) that **map** has only one parameter, which is the 'curried way' to look at **map**. Expressions like that are also called *partial application* of a function.

One aspect should be emphasised at this occasion: Since infix operators (like ∗) are functions as well (it is (∗) :: **Num** a ⇒ a → a → a), they can be treated in the same (curried) way. The multiplication operator is a function that takes one number as its argument and returns a function that multiplies another number to the first. Any infix operator can be written in prefix form by putting parentheses around it. Thus, it is legal

---
[4] The reader may guess whom this is named after.

to write the expression (∗) 2 which is the function that doubles its argument. This, in turn, implies that our declaration of double is equivalently given by:

```
double :: Integer → Integer
double = (∗) 2
```

The partial application of an infix operator is called a *section* and can also be written as the following equations convey:

$$(x+) = \lambda y \to x+y$$
$$(+y) = \lambda x \to x+y$$
$$(+) = \lambda x\ y \to x+y$$

Thus,

```
double :: Integer → Integer
double = (∗2)
```

is another possibility to declare our double function.

The following definition of **filter**, which is repeated for convenience, introduces a notation for *guards* (written behind a vertical bar) that allow for including conditional expressions into pattern matching:

```
filter :: (a → Bool) → [a] → [a]
filter p [] = []
filter p (x:xs)
    | p x = x : filter p xs
    | otherwise = filter p xs
```

When the pattern p (x:xs) matches, i.e., when **filter** is called with a function p as its first and a list (x:xs) as its second parameter, the conditional expressions written in the last two lines are evaluated one after the other, until one of them evaluates to **True**. The first conditional is p x which is the function call of p on x. The conditionals are separated from an expression by the equals sign (=). The 'predicate' p is the function that was passed to **filter** as its first parameter. It is of type a → **Bool**. If it evaluates to **True** for the given head element x, then the result of **filter** is declared to be the list that has the head element x and the tail given by **filter** p xs. That is, x is kept in the resulting list, and the **filter** function is applied recursively to the remainder of the list.

The second conditional expression is the predefined constant function **otherwise** which simply equals to **True**. Thus, because it is written as the last of the conditional expressions, this one always matches when the first one does not, and the result of **filter** is just the recursive application of itself to the remainder of the list, *without* keeping x.

Guards are, in the course of pattern matching, evaluated in the same sequence as they appear in the source code, and the first 'match' (equality with **True**) prescribes that the expression written to the right of the corresponding = is to be taken as the result. If no guard matches (which may happen in the general case, but not in our definition of **filter**), the evaluation continues with the next pattern.

All in all, **filter** produces a list of all those elements that satisfy the predicate given as its first parameter. Or, to pronounce it in a curried way, **filter**, when given a function as parameter that maps some value of type a to either **True** or **False** (let us call this function p), produces a *function* that will go through a given list of as and will keep only those list elements that yield **True** when put into the function p. Thus, if we had a function **odd** of the type **Integer** → **Bool** that returned **True** if and only if the given integer is odd (in fact, a function of that name and behaviour is indeed defined in the Prelude), the expression **filter odd** actually denotes the *function* that keeps all odd values in a given list of integers. Therefore, the expression (**filter odd**) [1,2,3] evaluates to [1,3]. Note that the parentheses have only been used to emphasise the 'function-ess' of **filter odd** and that they are not really necessary. The expression **filter odd** [1,2,3] is semantically equivalent, but makes us think of **filter** having two parameters. When reading (or writing) a Haskell program, one can always choose which pair of glasses one wishes to wear: the 'functions have one parameter' or the 'functions have many parameters' one. Luckily enough, one may change the pair at any time, back and forth, without any glitches.

Before closing this section of 'Haskell by Examples', we shall have a short look at one complete Haskell program. The definitions provided so far were just loose fragments of code; the following piece of code is a proper Haskell program that can be compiled and run:

File: Main.hs

```
module Main where

double :: Integer → Integer
double = (∗) 2

someOdds = (filter odd) [1,2,3]

main = putStr ( "All␣odd␣numbers␣in␣[1,2,3]␣are:␣"
        ++ show someOdds
        ++ "\nDoubling them yields: "
        ++ show (map double someOdds)
        )
```

The program is a **module** called Main and it consists of the three declarations for double, someOdds and main. The result of the whole program is given by the definition of main. It makes use of the function **putStr** that outputs a given string (the output is normally redirected to the standard output (stdout) of the environment that executes the program[5]). The string is the concatenation of two constants and two function calls. The expression **show** someOdds returns a string representation of the value of someOdds, which is the string "[1,3]" (without the quotes). Likewise, the second call to **show** produces the string "[2,6]".

It is without much surprise that one experiences the output of the program to be

---

[5] cf. section 3.3 on page 45 for a full explanation of input/output

```
All odd numbers in [1,2,3] are: [1,3]
Doubling them yields: [2,6]
```

3.2 Functions and types

The previous section already mentioned many aspects of Haskell and introduced many terms in the course of commenting on several code examples. In this section, we will strictly focus on functions and, especially, on the type system, going a little bit more into the details and highlighting important backgrounds.

3.2.1 Functions

Haskell is all about functions and expressions. Functions are first-class objects, i.e., they can be arguments of higher-order functions and they can be results of other functions. Both facts were demonstrated during the explanation of **map** and **filter** in the previous section. In an expression, the function application f x (with f being the name of a function and x being any expression) *applies* f to x. Function application is left associative, so that f x y means (f x) y (think 'curriedly').

In this context, it may be interesting to learn how to do function *composition* in Haskell. It can be achieved by the function composition operator '.' (dot). The operator is defined by the following *type signature* and declaration (quoted from the Prelude):

```
(.) :: (b → c) → (a → b) → (a → c)
f . g =  λ x → f (g x)
```

Thus, f . g denotes the function that first applies g, then f. Note that function application binds stronger than the dot-operator, so f . g x is equivalent to f . (g x) and not, as one perhaps might have intended, to (f . g) x. In order to save the parentheses, one can use the right-associating infix application operator $ and write f . g $ x, which is equivalent to (f . g) x, due to the low precedence level of $.

Functions in Haskell are *non-strict*. 'A function f is said to be strict if, when applied to a nonterminating expression, it also fails to terminate.' [HPF99, section 3.3] A nonterminating expression is equivalent to an expression that evaluates to an *error* or ⊥ ('bottom'). Errors are unrecoverable. Having non-strict functions means that function evaluation is performed *lazily*, in that (see [Tho99, p. 340])

- arguments to functions are evaluated only when necessary;

- arguments may be evaluated only partially;

- an argument is evaluated at most only once.

Consequently, with

```
three :: Integer → Integer
three x = 3
```

it is legal to evaluate the expression three (1/0), which yields 3, because the (erroneous) argument to three is never evaluated. The same holds for the evaluation of three bot where

```
bot = bot
```

Here, bot is a non-terminating expression, but three bot gives 3 nevertheless.

Laziness also allows for defining infinite data structures, especially lists, such as

```
threes = 3 : threes
numsFrom x = x : numsFrom (x+1)
allOdds = map (λx → x * 2 − 1) (numsFrom 1)
```

Here, threes creates an infinite list of 3's, numsFrom creates an infinite list that starts with a given value and continues with all its successors, and allOdds creates the infinite list of all odd integers.

Haskell provides a convenient syntax to denote infinite lists that contain sequences of numbers by specifying the first two values: one writes [n, m ..]. The difference m−n is subsequently added to calculate all successors. If m is omitted, the difference is considered to be 1 (one). Thus, the following three definitions yield equivalent values to those above:

```
threes = [3, 3 ..]
numsFrom x = [x ..]
allOdds = [1, 3 ..]
```

Combining list comprehension with recursion allows to conveniently define the infinite list of Fibonacci numbers (from [HPF99, section 3.3]):

```
fib = 1 : 1 : [ a+b | (a,b) ← zip fib (tail fib) ]
```

where the standard function **tail** returns the tail of a list, and **zip** returns the pairwise interleaving of its two list arguments:

```
zip (x:xs) (y:ys) = (x,y) : zip xs ys
zip   xs    ys   = []
```

The definition of fib 'works' because the definition itself only recurs to the first two elements of the list to be constructed: **zip** only needs the head of both of its arguments, and both are properly supplied by fib and **tail** fib due to the fact that the first two elements (two 1's) are already provided. With them, the next element can be calculated, and so forth.

3.2.2 Types

In Haskell, there is a strict separation between values and *types*. Any expression has an associated type. Due to the static type system, the type of any expression can be automatically inferred. Even more importantly, this can be done at *compile-time*, so typing errors are can be reported by the compiler even before the program is actually executed.

A type defines a set of values. The set contains all possible values that have this particular type.

Types are, in contrast to functions and values, no first-class objects. They cannot be used in normal expressions or passed along as arguments, and they are syntactically treated as a concept of their own. We already introduced *type expressions* informally in section 3.1.2, and we shall not go into much deeper detail here. Suffice it to say that type expressions describe types by combining type constructors (the unit type (), the list constructor [], the function constructor ($\rightarrow$), the tupling constructors (,), (,,), and so on, and user-defined type constructors) with concrete *type applications* (applying type constructors to type expressions). The function, tuple, and list constructors may be written in a more convenient syntax:

a $\rightarrow$ b	is equivalent to	($\rightarrow$) a b
(a,b,c)	is equivalent to	(,,) a b c
[a]	is equivalent to	[] a

This is the same syntax that would be used in normal expressions of the mentioned types, which is intentional. For example, the expression (e_1, e_2) has the type (t_1, t_2).

The existence of type variables in type expressions empowers us to describe *polymorphic types*, i.e., types that are universally quantified over type variables. Polymorphic types are *families* of types. When a type is seen as a set containing all possible values (instances) of a given type, a polymorphic type is a refineable description of a type. For example, in the type expression [a] (read: list of as), the type variable a, which matches any type, makes [a] actually denote all types that can be formed by homogeneous lists. Thus, the types **[Int]** (list of integers), **[Char]** (list of characters), **[Int $\rightarrow$ Char]** (list of functions that map integers to characters) and **[[a]]** (list of homogeneous a-lists) are subsets of [a]. Thus, one can deduce that the expression [1,2,3] (a list containing the first three integers) has the type **[Int]** *as well as* the type [a]. Clearly, the former is less general than the latter. In Haskell, each expression is guaranteed to have a *unique principal type*, which is the least general type that contains all instances. For any given expression, its unique principal type can be derived automatically.

The remainder of this section shows how to actually define new types. Similar to the separation suggested in §4 of the Language Report, the following subsections introduce *type classes* and *overloading*, *algebraic datatype* declarations, *type synonym* declarations, and *datatype renamings*, respectively.

Type Classes and Overloading

Type classes in Haskell ease the way of handling overloading or *ad hoc polymorphism*. The concept of a *class* in Haskell is different to that in an object-oriented language, where classes *are like* types, in that they contain objects [Tho99, p. 448]. A type class in Haskell *is made up of types*. In Haskell, a type class (or just *class*; the terms are used synonymously in [JH98]) declares which overloaded operations (called *class methods*) an instance of this class (i.e., a type) must provide. Since these operations are then known to be present for every type, the same operator identifier (or symbol) can be used *polymorphically* for values of many different types, and the 'correct' implementation can be inferred via the type system.

Classes are introduced by a *class declaration*:

```
class MyNum a where
  (+) :: a → a → a
  negate :: a → a
```

This states that the class MyNum comprises any type a for which the two operations + and **negate** (with the given signatures) are defined. Those types are called *instances*.

An *instance declaration* declares some type to be an instance of a class:

```
instance MyNum MyInt  where
  x + y = myAddInt x y
  negate x = myNegateInt x
```

Here, myAddInt and myNegateInt represent user-defined functions that do the actual adding and negating, respectively. The type MyInt must be defined elsewhere. The instance declaration then allows for using the operator + and the function **negate** on any value that has the type MyInt. This holds for *any* type that is declared to be an instance of MyNum, so the two operations can be polymorphically applied in any of these. For one concrete application, the 'correct' implementation is always applied automatically, because the type of the values can be inferred by the compiler.

The Prelude defines a plethora of classes and instances. Two of them already popped up in the previous section: **Eq** and **Ord**. Here are the definitions from the Prelude:

```
class Eq a where
  (==), (≠) :: a → a → Bool
  x ≠ y  =  not (x == y)
  x == y  =  not (x ≠ y)

class (Eq a) ⇒ Ord a where
  compare :: a → a → Ordering
  (<), (≤), (≥), (>) :: a → a → Bool
  max, min :: a → a → a
```

The class **Eq** describes types whose values may be compared for equality and for inequality. Strictly speaking, it describes types for which two functions == and ≠ are defined that map two values of type a to a **Bool**; the semantics is *not* specified by the class declaration (this is like the concept of an *interface* in other programming languages, e.g., in Java). Note, however, that *default methods* are provided, i.e., implementations that will be used when no declaration for the corresponding overloaded operator is provided by an instance. This indeed *does* add semantics to the declaration. In this particular case, since the definitions depend on one another, at least one of the default methods must be redefined by the instance. Default methods are completely optional, however (the default methods for **Ord** were omitted in the listing for the sake of brevity).

The class declaration for **Ord** introduces the notation used for defining *class extensions*: The *class assertion* **Eq a** in front of the arrow makes **Eq** a *superclass* of **Ord**. Haskell allows *multiple inheritance* (i.e., more than one superclass), provided that the generalisation relation is not cyclic.

Apart from declaring type classes that represent sets of types, one can also define classes that comprise type *constructors*. These classes are called *constructor classes* and will be explained in section 3.3 with the help of an example, namely the constructor class **Monad**.

Algebraic Datatype Declarations

One can define abstract data types with the help of the **data** keyword:

```
data MyBool = MyFalse | MyTrue
```

This introduces a new type MyBool with two 'values'. These values are represented by the two nullary *data constructors* MyFalse and MyTrue. Here, MyBool is a (nullary) *type constructor*. Data constructors can be used as patterns.

A slightly more complex example is the type for a binary tree with inner nodes and leaves:

```
data Tree a = Leaf a | Branch (Tree a) a (Tree a)
```

The type Tree a is a polymorphic type due to the type variable a. The types of the two data constructors are

```
Branch :: Tree a → a → Tree a → Tree a
Leaf :: a → Tree a
```

One additional feature is the possibility to attach *labels* to constructor fields:

```
data TripDescriptionRecord = TripDescriptionRecord
    { originCity :: City
    , destinationCity :: City
    }
```

Here, the two arguments originCity and destinationCity to the constructor TripDescriptionRecord are *labelled*, which makes it possible to access the respective parts by their name, and not only by their position. Note that the labels also serve as functions to *retrieve* a value from a given expression of type TripDescriptionRecord. For example, the first argument declaration implicitly defines the function originCity :: TripDescriptionRecord → City.

Type Synonym Declarations

The keyword **type** is used in *type synonym declarations* like

```
type Values = [Int]
type Point2D = (Float, Float)
type IntTree = Tree Int
```

'Type synonyms are a convenient, but strictly syntactic, mechanism to make type signatures more readable.' [JH98, §4.2.2]. They are commonly used to define shorter or more mnemonic names for types. A type synonym and its definition are, in principle, completely interchangeable[6]. Thus, a type synonym is no *new* type, but just a syntactic abbreviation.

Datatype Renamings

A *datatype renaming* introduces a new type whose representation is the same as an existing type. The only difference to a type synonym is the fact that a datatype renaming really creates a new type. This makes it possible to create a distinct instance of a class with different operations, which would not be possible if the two types were just synonyms. The corresponding keyword is **newtype**:

```
newtype IntTree = Tree Int
```

In contrast to the type synonym declaration for IntTree shown above, the declaration using **newtype** creates a distinct new type.

3.3 Monads

'It is useful to think of a monad as a strategy for combining computations into more complex computations.' [New05]. In Haskell, *monads* are used to be able to influence the order of evaluation of expressions. With monads, one can define *sequences* of expressions and gains a possibility to incorporate 'impure' code into a functional program. This is especially important when considering Haskell programs that do input and output (I/O). Without sequencing, their behaviour would be unpredictable. Monads provide a way of thinking in *actions* (or *(side-)effects*) returning values and the chaining together of these actions. Abstractly, an effect is something that represents a *state*.

A monad is a family of types m a, based on a type constructor m. A monad must comprise an operation *unit* (called **return** in the corresponding Haskell class), and an operation *bind* (called >>= in Haskell). One can think of a monad as being a container that holds a state (i.e., a value of some type a). The unit (**return**) operation turns a value into the appropriate corresponding monad value. The bind (>>=) operation applies a function from the value type a to the monadic type m a, thus defining a transition from one state

---

[6] except in instance declarations, see [JH98, §4.3.2]

to the next. The implementation of the bind operation actually defines the combination strategy by telling *how* to create a sequence of two actions. One can also say that it *binds* the value in the monad to the argument of the function that is to be applied.

The Prelude offers this class **Monad**:

```
class Monad m where
    (>>=) :: m a → (a → m b) → m b
    (>>) :: m a → m b → m b
    return :: a → m a
    fail :: String → m a
```

This declaration makes **Monad** a *constructor class* (in contrast to a normal type class), because m is used as a type constructor rather than a type. One can infer this from the signatures of the operations, where m is subsequently applied to a second type variable a to yield the type m a. This means that m must be instantiated with a one-ary type constructor[7]. Thus, being a constructor class, **Monad** demands its instances to be type constructors rather than types.

As was already said, a monad is a family of types m a, where m is a polymorphic type constructor and a is any type. Thus, since any polymorphic type can be regarded as being a container that may hold values of many different types, a concrete monad m a turns out to be a container of some type m holding values of some type a.

The operators >>= and >> define the sequencing of two actions. The bind operation >>= receives a monad of some type m a and a function that transforms a value of type a into a new monad of some type m b. In the standard case, the monads will be of the same type, i.e., a and b will be equal. The operation >> works similar to >>= in that it defines a transition from one monad to another, but here, no function is applied and the state in the first monad is simply forgotten. It is defined in terms of >>= as follows:

```
n >> k = n >>= (λ _ → k)
```

The operation **fail** can be overloaded to define a specific behaviour for failure.

Instances of **Monad** are supposed to give declarations for **return** and >>= so that the following equations hold:

$$
\begin{aligned}
\textbf{return } a >>= k &= k\ a & (1) \\
n >>= \textbf{return} &= n & (2) \\
n >>= (\lambda x → k\ x >>= h) &= (n >>= k) >>= h & (3)
\end{aligned}
$$

Axiom (1) states that **return** is a left-identity with respect to >>=, (2) states that **return** is also a right-identity with respect to >>=. Taken together, the first two axioms prescribe that **return** does not 'change' anything 'inside the monad', i.e., it does not create a new state. Axiom (3) states that >>= is associative.

It was not necessary to explicitly provide any 'extension' to the Haskell language itself to make it support monads. In order for the concept to work, it is important that all implementing interfaces stick to the three laws, a fact that cannot be checked by the

---

[7] That is, m is of *kind* $* → *$.

Haskell compiler. The Haskell language does, however, provide the **do** notation that makes monadic operations easier to use syntactically, but this is just for mere convenience. In addition, the Prelude contains many auxiliary functions and classes for the usage of monads.

Before showing the **IO** monad that handles input/output, let us have a short look at a simpler one: the **Maybe** monad.

First of all, the Haskell Prelude provides an abstract datatype **Maybe**:

```
data Maybe a = Nothing | Just a
```

This type is useful for dealing with illegal or optional values. Consider, for example, an hierarchical relation on web pages[8]. Every page, except the homepage, has exactly one parent page. This relation could be modelled by the function parent:

```
parent :: WebPage → Maybe WebPage
```

The result of parent is either **Nothing** (for the homepage, which is the root of the hierarchy) or it is the corresponding parent page, 'wrapped' by the **Just** constructor. If we want to apply parent multiple times, in order to, say, determine the grandparent page of a given page p, we have to consider the case where p does not even have a parent in the first place:

```
grandparent :: WebPage → Maybe WebPage
grandparent page = case (parent page) of
    Nothing → Nothing
    Just x → parent x
```

This differentiation is necessary for every additional hierarchy level that we want to step upwards to, if we wanted functions like grandgrandparent and so forth:

```
grandgrandparent :: WebPage → Maybe WebPage
grandgrandparent page = case (parent page) of
    Nothing → Nothing
    Just x → case (parent x) of
        Nothing → Nothing
        Just y → parent y
```

One idea might be to let each additional function call the previous one, so grandgrandparent would rely on grandparent. However, it is an even better solution to come up with a generalised function that abstracts this repetitive step:

```
oneStep :: Maybe a → (a → Maybe b) → Maybe b
oneStep Nothing _ = Nothing
oneStep (Just p) f = f p
```

The oneStep function is parameterisable with an operation that determines one single traversal step. In our example, we only have one operation of this kind: parent. Note that oneStep does not even have any reference to the WebPage type; it works for any type that is wrapped into **Maybe**. Now, we can write:

---
[8] The example is inspired by the sheep example in [New05].

```
grandgrandparent :: WebPage → Maybe WebPage
grandgrandparent page = oneStep (oneStep (Just page) parent) parent
```

The equation looks more intuitive when oneStep is written in in-fix form:

```
grandgrandparent page = (Just page) `oneStep` parent `oneStep` parent
```

As we can see, oneStep is one abstract computation that applies a given function to a value of type **Maybe** a. The abstraction lies in the fact that the given function is applied only in the case where the value is not **Nothing**. Now, this is an example of a *bind* operation! This turns **Maybe** into a monad, if an appropriate *unit* (i.e., **return**) function existed and the three axioms were obeyed. And this is indeed the case: it is

```
instance Monad Maybe where
    Nothing >>= f = Nothing
    (Just x) >>= f = f x
    return = Just
```

The last equation makes **return** be just **Just**. Remember that the obligation of **return** was to convert any value into a monadic value, so the value is simply wrapped in a **Just** expression. The bind operation >>= is exactly what we had already defined in the oneStep operation. With these definitions, the monad axioms hold indeed:

(1) **return** a >>= k $\rightsquigarrow$ **Just** a >>= k $\rightsquigarrow$ k a

(2) n >>= **return** $\rightsquigarrow$ n >>= **Just**

$$\rightsquigarrow \begin{cases} \textbf{Just } a \rightsquigarrow n & \text{if n is } (\textbf{Just } a) \\ \textbf{Nothing} \rightsquigarrow n & \text{if n is } \textbf{Nothing} \end{cases}$$

(3) n >>= (λ x → k x >>= h) $\rightsquigarrow$ $\begin{cases} (\lambda x \rightarrow k\ x >>= h)\ a \\ \quad \rightsquigarrow k\ a >>= h & \text{if n is } (\textbf{Just } a) \\ \textbf{Nothing} & \text{if n is } \textbf{Nothing} \end{cases}$

which is equivalent to (n >>= k) >>= h, because

(n >>= k) >>= h $\rightsquigarrow$ $\begin{cases} k\ a >>= h & \text{if n is } (\textbf{Just } a) \\ \textbf{Nothing} >>= h \rightsquigarrow \textbf{Nothing} & \text{if n is } \textbf{Nothing} \end{cases}$

The definition of the >>= operator for **Maybe** as an abstraction over our oneStep operator can be used whenever a *sequence* of function applications on expressions of type **Maybe** shall be specified, such that the occurrence of a **Nothing** determines the final result to be **Nothing**, and **Just** values are passed through the functions in sequential order. For example, take the **lookup** function that retrieves a value for a given key from an association list, i.e., a list of tuples. Its signature is

```
lookup :: (Eq a) ⇒ a → [(a, b)] → Maybe b
```

If the given key is not present in the list, then **Nothing** is returned, otherwise one gets the requested value, wrapped by **Just**. If one wishes to operate on the value, e.g., calculate its length (assuming string values for an example), one does not need an explicit conditional expression. Just write

```
lookup "b" [("a","first"),("b","second")] >>= (return . length)
```

which yields **Just** 6, because the key 'b' is in the list, and the word second has 6 letters. Note that the end-result is of type **Maybe** again, and that the function to the right of the >>= operator must return a value of that type as well. Thus, one always 'stays inside the monad'.

Monads unveil their true power when it comes to computations that induce side-effects. With the help of monads, it is possible to create 'well-defined areas of impurity' inside purely functional code. Thus, one keeps the benefits of functionality and at the same time allows to escape into statefulness and sequentiality. The aspect of *input/output* is one prominent example where these advantages come in handy.

Haskell provides the family of datatypes **IO** a as an abstraction for input/output. A value of type **IO** a is a 'program' (action) that performs some input or output and returns a value of type a. For example, the pre-defined function

```
getLine :: IO String
```

reads one line of input. The function returns an object of type **IO String**, i.e., a string wrapped by the **IO** constructor.

Printing a line of text to the standard output is performed by

```
putStr :: String → IO ()
```

The return type deserves some notion: it contains the *unit type* (). This type contains exactly one value, which is also written as (). It is used here because the return value of **putStr** is of no relevance. However, the function *has* to return *something* (and it must be of the type **IO** a), so **IO** () is a reasonable solution.

The type **IO** is an instance of **Monad**, so single input/output operations can be chained together using >>=. The actual definition of the **IO** monad is platform specific. There are no functions that tamper with values inside the monad and there are no data constructors, making it a one-way monad, so that any side-effect is completely confined to the monad and may do no 'harm' to the functional remainder of the program. When evaluated, the expression

```
getLine >>= (λ x → putStr x)
```

reads one line of input and echoes this line to the standard output. The utilisation of the >>= operator ensures that the given sequence (read first, then write) is obeyed under all circumstances. Since the type of the expression is monadic (**IO** (), to be precise), it cannot be used outside a monadic context (there are no operators or functions that could handle it), so there is no way for it to interfere with the functional semantics governing the surrounding program. Any expression that wants to access the values coming in from the outside world has to be inside a monadic expression as well. This is not constraining us in any way, however, because inside a monadic expression, anything else can be used as well:

```
getLine >>= (λ x → getLine >>= (λ y → putStr (reverse (y++x)) >>= (λ _ → getLine)))
```

This expression reads two lines of input, outputs the reverse of the concatenation of the first to the second line, and finally reads one more line of input (which is not used for anything).

If not for this example, the reader may have recognised a slight tendency of the expressions to become quite hard to read (notwithstanding the superfluity of most of the parentheses in above expression due to the third monadic axiom). This is where the **do**-notation helps:

```
do
  x ← getLine
  y ← getLine
  putStr (reverse (y++x))
  getLine
```

This is semantically equivalent to the expression shown above. Using **do**, one can assign values to variables (←), and subsequent lines are implicitly connected with the >>= operator. The value of the whole expression is defined by the last line (which must be an expression). Note that, of course, the variables are scoped locally, and that each assignment to a variable of the same name creates a *new* variable of that name.

To conclude, here is a complete Haskell program with input and output:

```
countInputLines :: IO Int
countInputLines = do
  line ← getLine
  if (length line) == 0
    then return 1
    else countInputLines >>= λ x → return (1+x)

main = do
  n ← countInputLines
  print n
```

The function countInputLines reads one line of input. If its length turns out to be zero, the result of the function is 1 (note the **return** operation from the monad class). If at least one character was typed, the function is called recursively and the result is one plus the result of this call. All in all, the functions counts how many lines are provided via standard input, until one empty line is received, which makes the recursion stop. In an imperative program, this would have been expressed with a **do**..**while** (Java) or **repeat**..**until** (Pascal) loop.

The example makes it apparent that the main variable that defines the overall result of the whole program is also of type **IO** (). Therefore, the **do** notation can be used here as well. For comparison and to show off that one can mix both notations freely, the **else** part in the countInputLines function is written without **do**.

3.4 Graphs

Their versatility and the ease of their use makes *graphs* an almost natural choice for modelling, storing and retrieving structured (or semi-structured) data. In the context of the web site generation and web site updating tasks that are covered in the course of this text, graphs will be used for different purposes whenever there is a possibility to do so. The current section will deal with the problem of representing graphs in functional languages (particularly, in Haskell) by reporting on the approach taken by Martin Erwig that will be adopted for the implementation described in this text.

3.4.1 Inductive Graphs

In [Erw01], Martin Erwig describes graphs as inductively defined data structures that are represented as terms. '[A] graph is either the empty graph or a graph extended by a new node v together with its label and with edges to those of v's successors and predecessors that are already in the graph. The representation of each edge contains the successor/predecessor node and the label of the edge. This information about a one-step inductive graph extension is contained in a type called the *context*.' [Erw01, p. 473]

Using this definition, it is possible to create directed labelled graphs. The following Haskell code, quoted from [Erw01], defines the algebraic type Graph:

```
type Node = Int
type Adj b = [(b, Node)]
type Context a b = (Adj b, Node, a, Adj b)
data Graph a b = Empty | Context a b & Graph a b
```

Nodes are represented by integers, as the first line suggests. One could easily substitute any other type for the nodes, but the idea of having *typed nodes* (i.e., different types for different nodes) is not considered in Erwig's paper.

The next line defines an adjacency list over some edge label type b as being a list of pairs of edge labels and nodes.

The third line gives the definition of a context, which is that amount of information necessary to extend a given graph by one additional node. The Context type is parameterised with a node label type (type variable a) and an edge label type (type variable b). The context then is actually a four-tuple $(pred, node, nodeLabel, succ)$ with the list of predecessor nodes, the new node, the new node's label, and a list of successor nodes. Note that the predecessor and successor node lists only contain nodes that are already contained in the graph being extended by this context.

The last line finally defines the data type itself. A graph with some node label type a and some edge label type b is either empty or it is the extension of an existing graph by some context. Note that the constructor function for the second case is &, written in infix form.

According to this definition, one can write terms that represent graphs. For example

```
([],1,'a',[]) & Empty
```

denotes a graph with a single node labelled a. The node is represented by the integer 1. This graph uses characters (**Char**) for the node label type. Adding a second node and one edge makes the term look like so:

```
([], 2, 'b', [("toA", 1)]) & ([],1,'a',[]) & Empty
```

This adds a node labelled b that has no predecessors, but one outgoing edge, itself labelled toA, going to the first node with label a.

Edges are labelled with **String**s, thus the graph is of the type Graph **Char String**.

The author of [Erw01] also provides a complete Haskell implementation of the definitions quoted so far. The *Functional Graph Library (FGL)*[9] consists of a comprehensive set of functions and a concrete implementation of the graph data type that is tuned towards efficiency. While being conceptually consistent with the ideas presented in the paper, the implementation uses type classes instead of algebraic types to represent graphs. The class Graph demands a set of functions (empty, isEmpty, match, mkGraph, labNodes) that can be used to define static (immutable) graphs. The class DynGraph is derived from Graph and adds the & 'constructor' function allowing to describe dynamic (expandable) graphs.

3.4.2 Data Type for Attributes

Using the FGL, one can define labelled, directed graphs. In order to store *type information* for nodes and edges as well as attributes and their values, the node and edge labels are instrumented to serve as a container for both. To this end, we define the type class AttributedLabelClass and one instance AttributedLabel. An attributed label wraps a dictionary that maps values to keys. The definition is as follows:

```
data AttributedLabel = Attributes (Map.Map Key Value) | NoAttributes
```

This data type will be used as the label type for nodes and edges. A label can either reference attributes (using the constructor Attributes), or it can be empty, expressed with the NoAttributes constructor. The actual attributes are represented by a dictionary that relies on the standard data type Map. We will constrain ourselves to using simple strings for keys as well as for values:

```
type Key = String
type Value = String
```

One special attribute for any node or edge is used to store the respective graph element's type. This attribute must have the key 'TYPE'. The name of the type is the value of that attribute.

In order to conveniently access attributes, the following type class is defined:

---

[9] The library is part of the *Haskell Hierarchical Libraries*, a standard set of packages distributed with common Haskell interpreters and compilers (package Data.Graph.Inductive.Graph in GHC).

```
class AttributedLabelClass a where
   fromList :: [(Key, Value)] → a
   toList :: a → [(Key, Value)]
   hasAttr :: a → Key → Bool
   getValue :: a → Key → Value
   setValue :: a → Key → Value → a
```

The four functions define an interface for attribute dictionaries that allows to create an initial dictionary from a list of key/value tuples (fromList), to test whether a given attribute exists (hasAttr), to retrieve the value of a given attribute (getValue), and to update the value of a given attribute (setValue). Note that the attribute dictionary is indeed update-able. Any 'change' to the dictionary that happens after its initial creation (using the setValue function) is represented by a new, modified version of that dictionary.

The interface is met by the AttributedLabel data type with the definition of corresponding overloaded functions, that effectively use already existing functions for the Map datatype in order to achieve the desired results.

```
instance AttributedLabelClass AttributedLabel where
   fromList l = Attributes (Map.fromList l)
   toList (Attributes a) = Map.foldWithKey (λk x ks → (k,x):ks) [] a
   toList (NoAttributes) = []
   hasAttr (Attributes a) k = (Map.member k a)
   hasAttr (NoAttributes) k = False
   getValue (Attributes a) k = (Map.!) a k    -- index operation
   setValue (Attributes a) k v = Attributes (Map.adjust (λ_ → v) k a)
   setValue (NoAttributes) k v = Attributes (Map.singleton k v)
```

In the following, graphs will be assumed to be of the type

```
Gr NodeType EdgeType
```

with

```
type NodeType = AttributedLabel
type EdgeType = AttributedLabel
```

The datatype Gr, defined in the FGL, is an instance of the class Graph, giving a concrete implementation of the basic graph functions (s.a.), based on trees.

The example graph for the TAS (cf. figure 11.4) is defined by the following declaration:

```
tas :: Gr NodeType EdgeType
tas = mkGraph
   [ (1, (fromList [("TYPE", "Customer"), ("name", "Alice")]))
   , (2, (fromList [("TYPE", "TransportationMethod"), ("id", "train")]))
   , -- and so on
   ]
   [ (1, 6, NoAttributes)
   , (11, 8, fromList [("TYPE", "to")] )
```

```
  , -- and so on
  ]
```

The function `mkGraph` (from the FGL) constructs a graph from a list of nodes and a list of edges, each given by a list of tuples. Nodes are represented by a unique integer number, which is the first element of a tuple, and a label, being the second tuple element. The label is, as was just pointed out, an attribute dictionary. The tuples that describe the edges contain the alpha and omega node (viz., the corresponding integer value), and the edge attributes.

3.4.3 Functions for Querying

The FGL provides a number of functions that allow for constructing graphs (e.g., adding nodes and edges), traversing them (e.g., performing a depth-first search), and for calculating graph properties (e.g., checking for connectedness). For our purpose, a more specific set of functions is desirable that know about node and edge attributes and thus can conveniently be used for *querying* the graph. It has to be admitted, though, that the term 'querying' possibly conveys too promising a connotation. We do not aim at providing a full-fledged query language. If greater flexibility and more expressive power is needed, one should resort to an existing querying language and use an appropriate API. In this light, the following functions are sufficiently helpful for the definition of the queries needed for the examples introduced in this text, but obviously there is room for further improvement. Due to the fact that, when following our approach, the queries themselves are separated from their actual usage in the page functions, extending or even replacing the querying facilities is a feasible task.

A rather common scheme for querying a graph is selecting nodes via the description of paths. Starting from a given node or a set of nodes, one wishes to retrieve all nodes that are reachable by a path. The path itself is given by a predicate.

The following function, `query`, is a simplified version of a functional path expression evaluator. The main restriction of the function results from it accepting a *list of functions*, each explicitly describing one individual 'step' of a *sequential* computation. It is not possible to use iteration or alternatives, at least not directly. In contrast to regular path expressions, the path is not defined *declaratively*, but *operationally*.

```
query :: Graph gr ⇒ gr a b → [Node] → [gr a b → Node → [Node]] → [Node]
query g ns [] = ns
query g ns (f:fs)
    | null ns || Data.Graph.Inductive.Graph.isEmpty g = []
    | otherwise = query g (concat (map (f g) ns)) fs
```

The arguments to `query` are, for one, the graph and a list of nodes. This list of nodes (let us call it `ns`) represents the initial set of nodes. Each node in `ns` is the starting point of one path. The third argument is a list of functions (named `fs` in the following). These functions map one node to a list of nodes.

The algorithm behind query is as follows: apply the first function from the list fs to each node in ns and *combine* the resulting node lists by simply concatenating them. This yields a new node list. Recursively proceed with the next function from fs on this *new* list, until no more functions remain in fs. Thus, the list of functions defines the number of steps, and each step is exactly one function application for every node in the current node list.

Consider, for an example, the following call:

```
result = query tas [1] [suc, suc]
```

The example uses the tas graph, which is a small example graph with data about a travel agency system (TAS). This system will be presented in chapter 11. The graph is depicted in figure 11.4. Evaluation of result gives us all successor nodes of all successor nodes of node 1 (this is the node of type Customer with the name attribute set to Alice). The function suc is predefined in the FGL and computes, for a given node n, all nodes that are direct successors of n. Instead of suc, any other function can be used as well, as long as it describes how to compute a new list of nodes from a given single node.

In general, one wants to include only *specific* nodes during the subsequent steps. The selection of nodes is in most cases based on attributes or on the type of nodes. Therefore, the following three functions are provided that make these kinds of queries easier to write.

The *first function* is comparable to the *restrict* function from relational algebra (σ). Its purpose is to keep a node n in the resulting list if and only if the node has a given value v for some attribute k:

```
constrainByAttr :: (Graph gr, AttributedLabelClass a) ⇒
    String → String → gr a b → Node → [Node]
constrainByAttr k v g n =
    if (getValue (label g n) k == v) then [n] else []
```

The first argument is the attribute name (key), the second is the value the attribute should be equal to, the third is the graph, and the fourth is the node n to be considered. The function returns a list containing only the given node n if the attributes indeed has the given value, and it returns the empty list otherwise. The comparison for equality is done with the == operator on strings. The label function retrieves a node's label, i.e., its attribute dictionary.

Note that the graph and the node are the *last* two arguments. This is intentional, because it allows to conveniently use constrainByAttr in the function list argument of query:

```
customer = query tas [1] [constrainByAttr "name" "Alice"]
```

Used this way, that is, with just two string arguments, the function passed to query exactly has the requested signature gr a b → Node → [Node]. Such is the beauty of curried functions!

The *second function* lets us filter by node *types*. Since the type information is stored as a special attribute, we can simply recourse on constrainByAttr:

```
constrainByType :: (Graph gr, AttributedLabelClass a) ⇒
    String → gr a b → Node → [Node]
constrainByType = constrainByAttr "TYPE"
```

The *third function* is useful when the data that shall be reported by a query is not a list of nodes, but rather some derived information based on the nodes' attributes. This functionality compares to the *project* function from relational algebra (π). To achieve the desired result, the following function takes a graph, a function f mapping labels to a value of an arbitrary type c, and a list of nodes ns, and applies f to the respective label of every n in ns:

```
nodesToValues :: (Graph gr, AttributedLabelClass a) ⇒
    gr a b → (a → c) → [Node] → [c]
nodesToValues g f = map (f . (label g))
```

The function thus can be applied to the result of a call to query as a finishing step, to transform the resulting node list into a list of values from the application domain, that can then be further processed by the caller.

The definitions in sections 6.3 and 11.8 provide examples for the application of these functions.

Part II

Functional Web Site Specifications

Modelling Aspects

The preceding chapters introduced the problem domain of our interest, and they provided a broad view on the scenery. In particular, chapter 2 dealt with a variety of approaches and ideas that we deem relevant, in the sense that their investigation yields further insight into the specific problem of appropriately modelling web sites and of successfully applying functional approaches to alleviate the task of modelling and specification.

We now have gathered enough knowledge to be able to go forward one more step. This chapter, and those that follow, will introduce a new approach that *combines* the merits of what one might call the 'classical' model-driven approaches, and functional programming. We envision that both worlds are not separate, nor are they ignorant of one another. They may and should be used in concert for their mutual benefit. Therefore, the following section 4.1 will present an integrated view on web site modelling with functional specifications. This view combines a set of models, each being apt to capture one specific aspect of the overall big picture. Section 4.2 will briefly comment on a suggested methodology, and section 4.3 will define important terms. Section 4.4 introduces an example web site that will be used in the subsequent chapters. Each chapter will then account for an in-depth treatment of one respective model.

4.1 Models

Section 2.1 described a selection of model-driven web engineering approaches and presented a common, almost consensual multi-dimensional space (cf. figure 2.1) that allowed to distinguish between different perspectives on a particular web engineering project. The following aspects were considered:

- the separation of the content level, the hypertext level, and the presentation level;

- the separation of the structural and the behavioural parts;

- the different activities of the development and evolution process.

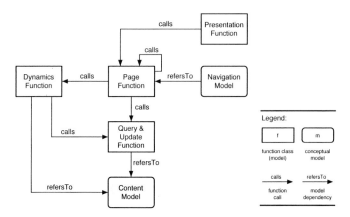

Figure 4.1: Integration of models and functions

In addition, a list of further concerns like customisation (the consideration of context information) or maintenance were pointed at.

We shall now present a set of *web engineering artefacts* that have to be delivered to form a complete description of a web site. Their presentation is compatible with the multi-dimensional space and the identified additional aspects, and it will be shown how the artefacts coherently fit into an overall model. Each artefact focusses on one respective key issue, namely

- defining a conceptualisation of the content (the content model);

- defining an abstraction layer for the access to the instance data by the means of querying (the query and update functions);

- defining the behaviour of the web site by declaring data processing functions (the dynamics functions);

- defining the composition of the single hypertext objects, i.e., the pages (the page functions);

- defining the navigation structure (the navigation model);

- defining the transformation of complete pages into a concrete output language (the presentation functions).

Figure 4.1 depicts the integration of the models and the functions. A white rectangle represents a class of functions, a shaded rectangle with rounded corners is a stereotype that represents a class of models. The two different kinds of symbols are merely used to improve readability. Arrows express that classes depend on one another. An arrow always points towards the 'dependee', i.e., an arrow between A and B signifies that A

depends on B. A function may call (calls) another function (thus, the first depends on the existence of the second), and a function may also refer to (refersTo) concepts defined in a model, and the page functions are referred to by the navigation model.

Before describing the artefacts one after the other in due detail, we will briefly introduce them in the following paragraphs, together with the general idea that lies behind the decision for this particular partitioning.

It is consensus to found the specification of a web site on a *content model*. This model captures the application domain by defining a conceptualisation, that is, the model identifies concepts and their relationships. The expression of the content model is achieved by using an UML class diagram, which offer a sufficiently rich set of notational elements. Once the content model is agreed upon, it can serve as a terminology for communication. And, even more importantly, the structure prescribed by the content model can be referred to by other artefacts that directly use the terminology defined therein. The actual instance data is a graph that complies to the content model. The content model is dealt with in chapter 5.

Some of these artefacts that use the content model are the *query and update functions*. The query functions define views on the instance data by referring to concepts from the content model. They introduce an additional level of abstraction by extending the terminology with new concepts that derive from the existing ones found in the content model. While query functions serve to *retrieve* instance data, the update functions are those that *apply changes* to it. All the details of query and update functions will be given in chapter 6.

The other artefacts that rely on the terminology offered by the content model are the *dynamics functions*. They define application-specific services that can be used to compose the application's behaviour. For a given web application, the dynamics functions cover the functional requirements of that application, and they are generally expressed in terms of the content model. The dynamics functions may use query and update functions to retrieve or change data in order to achieve the required result. They may also rely on services that reside *outside* the system. For further information, see chapter 7.

At the centre of a web application lie the hypertext documents. We will use *page functions* to define them. Page functions declare the composition of a page from page fragments, the incorporation of results from query functions, and the triggering of dynamics functions. Pages may include links to other pages. The result of a page function is a regularly structured algebraic term that conforms to the *abstract page description* data type (APD). This type does not induce any presentation-specific aspects. Since the function definition will be written using a functional programming language, and this definition *is* the construction of the APD term, the full power of the respective functional language can be utilised for that task. This offers quite some advantages, like the possibility to use higher-order constructs or templating techniques. A detailed treatment of page functions can be found in chapter 8.

The hypertext documents, i.e., the single pages, form a web of pages. The inherent structure of such a web site is modelled in the *navigation structure model*. This model defines a hierarchical backbone inter-page hyperlink system. The model also considers authorisation constraints that may be imposed on single pages or on sets of pages. A visual language will be presented for expressing concrete navigation structures. The definition of that language and everything else about navigation structure models is to be found in chapter 9.

It was already said that pages are defined in an abstract manner that does not refer to a concrete presentation language. In order to deliver pages, the APD term that represents a page will be transformed by a *presentation function*. A presentation function defines a mapping from the APD to an arbitrary output language. The mapping itself can be the same for every page, or it can be more elaborate by referring to context information or to data inside the respective page, so that it produces different outputs according to the current state of the system. This flexibility is necessary for the definition of customisable and adaptive web applications. Presentation functions will be described in chapter 10.

The correspondence of the six kinds of artefacts to the multi-dimensional space already shone through in the preceding explanations, but the relations should be emphasised at this point. The separation of the content level, the hypertext level, and the presentation level is achieved by using three different artefacts: the content model, the page functions, and the presentation functions, respectively. The separation of the structural and the behavioural parts of a web application is modelled by using dynamics functions for the specification of the application's behaviour, and the aforementioned artefacts to define the structural part.

The term *behaviour* here refers to the functional requirements, or, in other words, the business logic. In general, the behavioural aspect of a web application encompasses everything that changes during run-time, which may also include alterations to the content, hypertext, or presentation model. While we assume a *static* content model (the data itself may change at run-time, but the model, which corresponds to the schema level, may not), changes to the navigation structure are achieved by using conditional expressions to create new or hide existing links in the page functions, and the presentation is also apt to being changed at run-time by referring to the system state in conditional expressions.

4.2 Methodology

As will become apparent in the course of the presentation of the two example web applications, there is no fixed order of creating the models. The overall process is, after all, an iterative one, and the models are revised and extended during the development. We suggest relying on existing processes, and adapting them to the actual requirements of the web application project in question. Section 2.3 presented a brief overview on possible candidates.

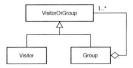

Figure 4.2: Visitors and groups of visitors

4.3 Terminology

Before starting with the description of the example, some terms have yet to be defined.

Visitors and Groups

The *web site visitor* is the individual who uses his or her web browser to access a web site. To a certain extent, however, it makes sense to take a more technical point of view and to abstract from the fact that there is a *person* involved who initiates page requests. In common terminology, the entity 'on the other end' is referred to as a *user agent*◇. It is a piece of software that speaks HTTP. In most cases, this will be a web browser, but it might as well be any other software, for example, a robot program gathering information on behalf of a search engine, or a web service application. In the following, we will use the term *visitor*◇ in its broadest sense so that it denotes both, the person *and* the software that does the actual communication with the web server.

Especially in the context of authorisation, it is convenient to define *groups* of visitors. The idea is to treat groups and individual visitors uniformly, so that, for example, permissions can be granted to a number of visitors in one single operation. This is specifically useful if the same set of visitors shall be granted certain permissions for *different* objects in the web site. If the composition of the group changes, this is automatically reflected at all places where this group is referred to. Without groups, one would have to perform corresponding changes at all those places individually.

The class diagram in figure 4.2 captures our notion of visitor groups. The three classes reflect the composite pattern ([GHJV94]). An individual visitor is modelled by the Visitor class, a group of visitors is captured by the class Group. A group may compose of individual visitors and other groups, which is signified by the aggregation association between Group and VisitorOrGroup. The latter class serves as the abstraction over groups and individual visitors. The multiplicity attached to the aggregation forbids empty groups.

Authorisation

The term *authorisation*◇ is used to denote the act of ensuring that a given web site visitor has the permission to perform a certain task. A *permission*◇ can be associated to any action that can be performed on an object. If the object is a web page, for example, then a permission called ViewPage might exist that is checked prior to showing the page. Thus, a permission defines *what* can be done with a particular object.

Permissions are not directly granted to visitors or groups of visitors, but to roles. A *role◇* is a collection of visitors. A visitor can have any number of roles. Thus, a role defines *who* can do something with a particular object.

Putting it all together, we want to relate an object to a permission and a role, thus expressing that all visitors who have a given role (*who?*) are entitled to perform a given action (*what?*) on the object in question.

4.4 The Computer Science Faculty Web Site

The explanation of the deliverable artefacts will refer to an example web site for illustration purposes. Whenever the presentation of concrete artefacts is considered useful in addition to the abstract definition of ideas, the chosen example is called into play: the web site of the Computer Science Faculty of Koblenz-Landau University. Since this web site only serves as a consistent point of reference throughout the following chapters, we will not present it as a complete web site project. Rather, we will only highlight specific parts of it as we proceed through the upcoming artefact descriptions, thus unveiling it piece by piece.

However, since it *does* make sense to provide a report on how to actually handle a complete web site development project, we will do so in chapter 11 for a travel agency system.

The Computer Science Faculty of Koblenz-Landau University recently launched its new web site[1]. It has just been re-designed and is still being extended with additional content. The site provides the visitors with many kinds of information of and about the faculty. The faculty web site is reachable from the Koblenz campus web site, which serves as an entry portal to the web sites of all four existing faculties and of further institutions on the Koblenz campus. Since there are no campus-wide agreements on how the faculty web sites should look like, the faculty of computer science, like the other faculties, autonomously decided upon the site's content, structure, and design.

Figure 4.3 shows the homepage of the Computer Science Faculty web site.

The next chapter will present the content model that builds the foundation of this web site.

---

[1] The homepage is located at http://www.uni-koblenz.de/FB4

Figure 4.3: Computer Science Faculty Homepage, http://www.uni-koblenz.de/FB4, as of 16/08/2005

Content Model

It is intentional that the content is mentioned as the first of the core topics. After all, almost every web site *is all about* content. At this point, it might be worthwhile to sharpen the differentiation between a web site and a web application. Although there is no clear borderline between the two – and thus it presumably does not make much sense to try and *precisely define* the terms – it can be stated that a web site is essentially *content-driven* and a web application is a web site that stresses *functionality*. Historically, web sites have their roots in document-centric hypertexts, an area with long tradition (confer Vanevar Bush's milestone vision in [Bus45]). The Web, as devised by Tim Berners Lee ([BL89], [BL99]), was an information medium, suitable to publish and globally access data in form of text and, later, images and other media types. It is only recently that more and more web sites can be labelled *applications*, which is a trend forced by the realisation of the usefulness of the web as a distribution channel for applications and the requirement to transfer traditional software 'to the Web.' These kinds of web sites can be regarded as user interfaces to (new or existing) applications, or they serve to integrate services, applications and document-centric data. We will continue to speak of web *sites* as the broader of the two concepts, meaning the term to subsume web applications unless otherwise stated.

In this light, it becomes clear that web sites, as well as web applications, include functionality, but essentially *live* from content, and that the content model is fundamental.

5.1 Application Domain Conceptualisation

A content model is the conceptualisation of the application domain. A *conceptualisation* comprises concepts from the universe of discourse, a 'functional basis set' and a 'relational basis set' (cf. [GN87, p. 9 ff.]). We will not regard the functional aspects at this time. Thus, as our working definition, we consider a conceptualisation to be the concepts (or entities) that are assumed to exist in some area of interest and the relationships between them. Thus, the model *identifies* (i.e., gives names to) concepts and relates the concepts to one another. Note that the conceptualisation contains the concepts itself, not just their names. The content model is expressed using an UML class diagram. It is common practice to use these kinds of diagrams for this particular purpose, because they provide a broadly accepted, well-defined, sufficiently rich syntax and they enjoy good tool support. As far as the semantics is concerned, opinions diverge. This, however, will not affect its usefulness and appropriateness for our modelling task, as we can get along quite well with the common understanding of what the diagrams mean, and without formalising this meaning. As soon as semantical issues become relevant in the explanations that follow, as will be the case when talking about the instance data, we will present them with 'just the right' level of formality.

As with any model, the chosen level of abstraction and the actual choice of concepts and relationships depends on the purpose of the model. A model is useful only with an accompanying statement about its purpose, or intention. Regarding the content model, this purpose is also allowed to change during the lifetime of the model: first versions of the content model might be intended as a communication medium and as a coarse-grained snapshot of the application domain, while later revisions might be directed towards specification or implementation. Together with the implications of the iterative process that is suggested, it should have become apparent that the content model will evolve over time, until it reaches the desired stability. In the following, we will abstract from this evolution and assume that the content model is in a stable state. Questions concerning the dynamics of the content model did already resurface near the end of section 4.1.

For some, it still seems to be an art rather than a technique to design an appropriate content model, and it is almost impossible to state general rules or procedures for deciding on which concepts to include. There are some rules of thumb, like considering the nouns in the available domain description documents ([Abb83], [HK99, p. 201]), and suitable training will help to gain a reliable degree of expertise. We will abstain from dealing with this very general problem any further. Suffice it to add that *re-using* models is often possible and also beneficial. As application domains possibly overlap, the same concept might be included in several content models, like, for example, the notion of a 'shopping basket'. This term is not specific to one application, but applies to many. Substantial effort is spent in creating commonly applicable ontologies, be they web-specific ([Mil05]), domain-specific (e.g., [Aum05]) or neither (e.g., [NP01]).

The conceptualisation laid down in the content model constitutes an agreement on a common language. This is important because all other artefacts, directly or indirectly, refer to and thus rely on the content model. They build further levels of abstraction by adding new concepts that are defined in terms of the original ones. As an example, consider the query functions (see section 6) that will be defined by declaring views on some instance data. Each query function has got a name of its own, thus becoming a new identifiable and usable concept. Some concepts are also provided by the system itself, that is, they do not appear in the content model, but in pre-defined function libraries. This includes, as an example, implementation related concepts like 'session' or 'user'.

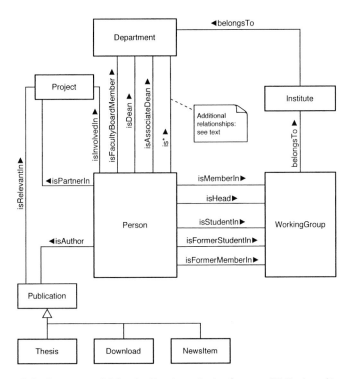

Figure 5.1: Content model for the Faculty web site (syntax: UML class diagram)

5.2 Content Model for the Example Web Site

This section deals with the content model for the computer science faculty web site. Figure 5.1 shows the corresponding UML class diagram.

The model has evolved tremendously during the development process. The version presented here is a simplified version of the one actually used in the current implementation. In the course of time, the model has quickly grown to a rather complete and very elaborate conceptualisation of the application domain. During the design phase, however, the model has been stripped down to a simpler version that contains just the classes needed for the implementation. The model is intended to capture all possible states of the system, and temporal aspects are not taken into account.

Note that the diagram in figure 5.1 depicts the classes without their attributes. They will be introduced in the following text instead.

A pivotal role can be attributed to the Person class, because almost every other concept is connected to it, either directly or indirectly. The reason for this is quite apparent, since people are the main topic of the web site. However, the model covers only a fraction of the information one would normally expect from a full-fledged information system that stores data about people. This is a further indication showing that the model is tailored towards a specific web application and thus only contains the information that is absolutely necessary. A person has a name and a unique id (attributes name and id) and one can store one URL per person designating the preferred 'home' page (attribute url).

A person can be related to a working group (WorkingGroup) in different roles, which are modelled by associations. He or she can be a staff member (isMemberIn), a student working for the group (isStudentIn), a former member or a former student (isFormerMemberIn, isFormerStudentIn, respectively) or the working group's head (isHead). A person can also be involved in a project (Project), either as participant (isInvolvedIn) or as partner (isPartnerIn). A working group has an id (attribute id) and a designation (attribute designation) that signifies its area of research, serving as the name of that working group. The group can also be referred to by the name of its head.

A working group belongs to (belongsTo) an institute (Institute). In rare cases, a working group may be affiliated to more than one institute, but normally this is an n-to-1 relationship. The members of an institute are implicitly given as the union of all working group members whose working group belongs to this particular institute. An institute has an id and a designation (attributes id and designation).

Each institute belongs to (belongsTo) a department[1] (Department). A department has a dean (isDean), an associate dean (isAssociateDean), as well as a number of boards, which are defined by relating persons to the department using the relationships isFacultyBoardMember as well as isGHRKOMember, isZFUWMember, isBibMember, isDiplMember, isHabilMember, isPromoMember, isLUSTMember, isRepreRoom, isRepreFacultyDay, isRepreGenderEquality. These relationships are symbolised by the is* relationship that was put in the diagram in order to keep it legible.

Publications (Publication) are another very important concept in this model. They are written by people (isAuthor). A thesis (Thesis) is a special kind of publication. A publication may be related to (isRelevantIn) a project, for example if this publication is a paper created in the context of the project. Every publication has an id and a title (attributes id and title).

The class NewsItem represents any kind of information that is attached to a given date, for example a singular event, or an announcement. It can convey a short note and a hyperlink to a page with more information. News items are categorised with simple strings, so it is possible to select them according to a list of categories.

Downloads (Download) are sets of files that can be made available for downloading. They can be used to share software products or other documents. It is possible to restrict the downloading to a set of authorised users.

---

[1] The terms *department* and *faculty* are used synonymously in this section.

Query and Update Functions

To *query* means 'to ask questions of [somebody,] especially with a desire for authoritative information.' [MW05, query (2, verb)] This definition is a good indication of what we want to subsume under this term: retrieving *authoritative* information from one *reliable* source by posing appropriate questions. A *question* in our context is a declarative description of the desired result, which is almost in stark contrast to how one would see this term defined in a standard dictionary, e.g., 'form of expression in speech or writing that requests an answer from [somebody]' in [Hor89, question (n)]. Instead of asking 'What time is it?', we say 'The answer is a time information x, in 24-hour format, such that x is equal to the current time of the day.' Please note that *both* version of the question are not precise in an absolute sense, although the second might look more elaborate. Missing precision is not a defect, however, because questions are – or at least should be – answered under a consensual set of presumptions. Asking for the current time, in either version, only renders the desired result if both the inquirer and the questioned source share a common notion of the concept 'time,' and if both assume that asking for it generally refers to the *local* time, for example. This underlines the importance of a well-defined set of context information and a well-defined conceptualisation.

Both question types are different in that the second version involves a predicative description of the result, whereas the first version conveys the structure of the result only implicitly. It were rather confusing, but absolutely reasonable, to answer 'What time is it?' with 'It's good!' This answer would not qualify for the second version of the question, however, because it does not fit into the description of the x imposed by the second version.

We will use the noun *query* to denote the questions we just talked about, that is, declarative descriptions of the desired result.

But it is not only queries that we are interested in. It is one thing to *obtain* some piece of information – in the context of web sites and web applications, it is equally important to *add* new pieces of information to the system, making them available for subsequent queries. Thus, the information space grows and evolves over time, which also involves the possibility of repeated queries to return varying answers, depending on what kinds of *updates* to the information base took place in the meantime.

Before considering the actual definitions of queries and updates in section 6.3, we have to describe the data that the queries and the updates are all about, which is the responsibility of section 6.1. Section 6.2 will introduce an additional level of abstraction to that data that will make query results more convenient to work with.

6.1 Instance Data

Instance data is all data that is considered part of the system that we are in the course of developing. The content model defines the interrelation of concepts, which are abstractions for sets of objects. The set of objects that is 'subsumed' by a concept is also called its *extension*, and the individual objects are *instances* to this concept. We can treat the instance data as being completely separate from the conceptualisation, so that the actual extensions are of no importance during modelling. This abstraction step is, after all, what conceptualisation is all about. The extensions only come into play when the system is actually set to run.

The instance data typically changes during run-time, which requires a non-static repository. As was already hinted at in section 3.4, *graphs* will be used for the representation of that data. This affects not only the structure of the internal storage, but also the interface to accessing the data. By using *typed* graphs, we gain coherence of the graph and the content model, which allows to access the graphs using terms that correspond to concepts in the content model. The remainder of this section will deal with both: the graph repository and its relationship to the content model.

6.1.1 Graph Repository

The instance data will be kept in a graph repository, that is, as nodes and edges. The graph class of our choice is TGraphs ([EWD+96]), which are typed, attributed, directed, and ordered graphs. This offers a very powerful expressiveness.

Nodes, as well as edges, have a type and an associated set of attributes. Attributes are named values. Edges in the graph may have a direction, and, for a given node, all incident edges have a persistent ordering.

At the implementation level, we will employ the same language for managing the graph repository as we use for accessing the data and incorporating it into the pages. Section 3.4 already introduced the functional graph library (FGL) that lets us seamlessly work with the graph in our chosen implementation language, Haskell.

The FGL does not support typed graphs, which seems to be a bit of a drawback. There is a remedy, however, so that the lacking type support does not disqualify the library. The idea is to attach type information to nodes an edges via a designated attribute that stores a type identifier. Thus, queries can refer to the type of a node or edge. This solution is no replacement for a 'real' type system, that should also, for instance, guarantee that graph elements of a given type actually have the set of attributes defined by the respective type,

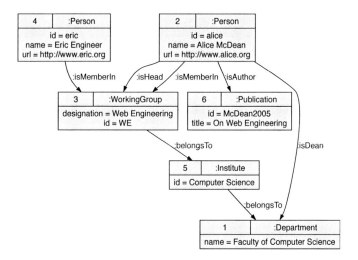

Figure 6.1: The example instance graph for the Computer Science Faculty web site (syntax: see text)

or provide functions to determine the set of *classes* a given graph element belongs to. For our examples, however, the available features suffice, and there is no need to resort to a different solution. In principle, any other library could have been used as well.

Example Graph

Let us look at the example graph for the Computer Science Faculty web site. It contains only a very limited amount of instance data, which helps in keeping the example simple and comprehensible.

The diagram in figure 6.1 visualises the example graph. It was created by outputting the Haskell representation into a file adhering to the DOT format [Dot05], using an output function that is provided as part of the FGL library, and finally rendering that file with the graph layout software GraphViz [EN05]. In the diagram, nodes are depicted by boxes. Each box contains the node number in the upper-left corner, the node's type in the upper-right corner, and attribute values are listed in the lower part of the box. Edges are annotated with their type.

The instance data represented by the graph comprises of information about two persons (Alice and Eric). Alice is the dean of the Faculty of Computer Science, and she also heads the Web Engineering working group. Eric is a member of this working group, which belongs to the Institute of Computer Science. There is one publication with the title "On Web Engineering", having Alice as its author.

6.1.2 Compliance to the Content Model

We already talked of the 'type' and 'class' of a node or edge, but did not explicitly say what this should mean. The point is that we regard the graph as being an *instance* of the content model. This thinking is inspired by the notion of a graph *schema*, as introduced in the $\mathcal{Z}$-based EER/GRAL approach (cf. [DEF$^+$98], [Spi92]). A graph schema, or, more precisely, an *EER schema* (extended entity-relationship schema), formally defines a type system, an incidence system, and an invariant system. A type system comprises a set of types that can be related to one another in a type/subtype relationship. Every type has one associated attribute schema, which is a mapping from attribute identifiers to a set of all possible values (the domain). An incidence system relates each relationship type to two entity types, so one can express that two given entity types are related under a particular relationship type. An invariant system allows to impose cardinality constraints on relationships, i.e., a minimum and maximum number of occurrences.

It is not our intention to go too much into the details of the definition of an EER schema, because a basic understanding should suffice in order to follow our argument. Some parts were omitted, but this abstraction step should improve rather than disrupt the explanations.

All components of an EER schema have a formal semantics that make an EER schema define a set of graphs, that is, a *graph class*. This is achieved by stating a definition for an 'is-instance-of' relation between a graph and a schema. This definition demands that node types and edge types of the graph comply to the type system given in the schema, that the incidences found in the graph adhere to the incidence system of the schema (i.e., that every edge of a given type connects two nodes that have the prescribed node types), and that the invariant schema is complied to as well.

In a nutshell: Given a typed, attributed, directed, ordered graph and an EER schema (i.e., a graph class), it can be checked (automatically, using mathematics), whether or not the graph is a valid instance.

This opens a new door when considering the following fact: one can correlate an EER schema and a content model. The expressiveness of both are sufficiently close to one another to let us produce a corresponding EER schema for any 'reasonable' content model. The adjective 'reasonable' conveys that not any *conceivable* content model fulfils the necessary requirements, but that normally one uses only those that do. The qualification depends on the UML features employed; simple class diagrams without OCL constraints are perfectly 'reasonable' in the above sense. A class in the content model corresponds to an entity type in the EER schema, an association corresponds to a relationship type or to a subtype-relation, and cardinalities can be mapped to a corresponding invariant system.

We use the graph and the content model in this spirit.

The language GRAL can be used to add constraints that are not expressible with an EER schema. GRAL is based on $\mathcal{Z}$ and provides predicates that are specifically suited for writing constraints on graphs elements. Since the GRAL semantics is specified formally, the conformance of a given graph to a given set of GRAL constraints can be checked automatically.

6.2 Data Type Definitions

A query defines a view on the instance graph. The query result is used in page functions to include the data in the actual web pages. Since the graph complies to the content model, the queries may also refer to concepts and relationships defined in that model, by using the *types* of nodes and edges. In order for the data to appear on a page, it must be converted to a form that is closer to the serial structure of a page. In principle, queries may produce results of arbitrary structural complexity, ranging from subgraphs, over complete nodes with attributes, to simple strings. Inside the pages, and also in other functions that operate on data returned by queries, a simpler schema is often asked for. To this end, we define an additional level of abstraction that reflects the view on the data as taken from the web pages, opposed to the conceptual view taken in the content model. Concretely, we compose the data into record-like structures that correspond to requirements that were imposed after deciding which data should be displayed on which page, and also how data shall be transferred between pages by using forms.

In addition to classes and relationships as defined in the content model, we use records and lists of records to model the navigational view on the data. The functions that will be using the queries will thus get a simpler, cleaner interface to the data, that is also much closer to the data structure needed in these respective functions.

Take, as an example, a page that is to list data about a person, comprising, say, the name of that person, an URL to the home page, and the name of the working group he or she is affiliated to. The query should be formulated according to the content model. The page that incorporates the person data, however, rightfully expects that it receives the *relevant* data only, in a format that is convenient to handle. One such format is a list of tuples that contain exactly the data that is used inside the page, and nothing more. In order to list the persons' names and home pages along with their respective working group, this involves returning just these three items per person, as opposed to a more complicated structure consisting of two connected nodes, one for a person and one for the working group, for example.

This allows for an additional level of abstraction that improves the conciseness of the functions that deal with query results, without forcing them to 'know' too much about the content model. It should be noted that the decision upon the elaborateness of this additional level is up to the designer, which offers great flexibility. In the course of an iterative design, this abstraction level, like the others as well, will evolve and eventually converge.

To start with, let us assume that a simple data type PersonRecord is available that can be used to store a person's name and an URL of the person's homepage:

```
data PersonRecord = PersonRecord
  { personId :: String
```

```
  , name :: String
  , url :: String
  } deriving Show
```

The same schema can be followed for working groups:

```
data WorkingGroupRecord = WorkingGroupRecord
  { workingGroupId :: String
  , designation :: String
  } deriving Show
```

In order to satisfy the aforementioned expectations of a page that only needs a person's name and the corresponding working group name, one could come up with:

```
data PersonNameAndWorkingGroupRecord = PersonNameAndWorkingGroupRecord
  { personName :: String
  , workingGroupDesignation :: String
  } deriving Show
```

∎

The type system induced by the content model is available only implicitly in the Haskell specifications, but the additional types like the ones shown above are written as proper Haskell types. This allows for compile-time type checking of the respective functions that refer to these types in their signatures, so that potential errors are spotted as early as possible.

The queries are tightly bound to the content model, and this is intentional and unavoidable. If the content model evolves, the queries have to be updated accordingly. These changes, however, are mostly confined to the queries themselves, and do not affect the additional higher levels, which is another argument in favour of their introduction.

6.3 Query Functions for the Example Web Site

For the Computer Science Faculty web site, a series of query functions will be used in the upcoming specifications. These query functions will be introduced in this section. They use the auxiliary graph accessing functions that were already described in section 3.4.3, so this section can constrain itself to explaining only those aspects that are unique to the examples.

As a matter of fact, there are no *update* functions necessary to specify the example web site. The reader is referred to the second example web site (the travel agency system), as described in chapter 11, for an application of graph updates.

6.3.1 queryPersonIdsByName

The following query returns the ids of all persons whose names start with a given prefix.

```
queryPersonIdsByName :: AttributedGraph → String → [String]
queryPersonIdsByName g name =
  nodesToValues
    g
    (λ lbl → getValue lbl "id")
    (query g (nodes g)
       [ constrainByType "Person"
       , constrainByAttrFun (isPrefixOf name) "name"
       ]
    )
```

The query starts by constraining the nodes to those of type Person. Of these, it retains those whose name attribute has the prefix that was passed as the second argument to the query function. In order to do this, the function **isPrefixOf**, defined in the standard prelude, is mapped over the nodes' attributes.

6.3.2 queryPersonById

The following query retrieves the data for one particular person, given the person's id.

```
queryPersonById :: AttributedGraph → String → Maybe PersonRecord
queryPersonById g personId =
  let
    records = nodesToValues
      g
      (λ lbl → PersonRecord
         { personId = (getValue lbl "id")
         , name = (getValue lbl "name")
         , url = (getValue lbl "url")
         }
      )
      (query g (nodes g)
         [ constrainByType "Person"
         , constrainByAttr "id" personId
         ]
      )
  in
    if (length records) == 1 then Just $ head records else Nothing
```

The query itself is rather basic. The definition in the **let** expression finds all nodes that are of type Person and whose id attribute equals the given parameter. In the erroneous cases that two persons exist with the same id or that no person with the given id could be found, the query functions returns **Nothing**. Otherwise, the constructed person record with the id, the name, and the url is returned.

6.3.3 queryWorkingGroupMembersById

The following query retrieves a list of members of a given working group.

```
queryWorkingGroupMembersById :: AttributedGraph → String → [PersonRecord]
queryWorkingGroupMembersById g wgId =
  nodesToValues
      g
      (λ lbl → PersonRecord (getValue lbl "id") (getValue lbl "name") (getValue lbl "url") )
      (query g (nodes g)
          [ constrainByType "WorkingGroup"
          , constrainByAttr "id" wgId
          , (λ g n → map fst                                                        (1)
              (filter (λ (n, l) →
                  getValue l "TYPE" == "isMemberIn") $ lpre g n)
          )
          ]
      )
```

This particular query deserves some further consideration, as it uses a non-standard function to calculate the desired list of person records in the expression beginning in the line marked with (1). Recall that each function in the list argument to the query function has to calculate a new list of nodes from a given node. To do so, the functions are called for each element in the list of nodes, and the resulting lists are concatenated to yield a new list of nodes, forming the input to the next function in the sequence. The lambda expression shown in the code above indeed fits into this scheme, and it performs the following task: It calculates all predecessors of the given node n via the function lpre, which returns a list of tuples of the form (Node, Label), where the first tuple element is a predecessor of n, and the second tuple element is the label, i.e., the attributes, of the *edge* between the two nodes. The resulting list is then filtered to retain only those node/label pairs that belong to an edge of type isMemberIn. Of these, we extract the first component, which is the node, by mapping the **fst** standard function over the list. In the end, the resulting list contains exactly the *persons* that are a member of the given working group.

Dynamics Functions

Dynamics functions help defining the business logic of a web application. This *behaviour* represents what the application shall actually *perform*. The dynamics functions thus are strongly connected to the functional requirements, especially those laid down in use case definitions or in the reports on concrete usage scenarios.

The more 'dynamic' a web site is, there is need for functions that help to master this additional level of complexity. It seems to be quite an ambitious endeavour to find a 'metric of dynamics' that entitled us to precisely measure a web application's performance in this dimension. When is one web site more dynamic than another? We therefore retreat to pursuing a qualitative approach. For us, it is sufficient to note that the 'amount' of dynamics may differ, and even substantially so, from application to application. Some might manage with only a few and simple functions, while others might involve complex functionality, combined with the dependency on external services. The terms web *site* and web *application* can be used to signify that the amount of dynamics is lesser or, respectively, higher. The differentiation is not a definite one, and the terms only pronounce a tendency, so in the end, both terms can also be used synonymously. The necessity for dynamics functions may be lower for some web sites, but the general ideas stay the same. Our approach is suitable for both kinds of applications.

Dynamics of a web site can be almost naturally modelled via functions.

This chapter will introduce the concept of dynamics functions, along with the necessary definitions that allow for their specification. Section 7.1 will relate on the idea of consulting the functional requirements as an inspirational source for dynamics functions. Section 7.2 concludes with an example.

7.1 Functional Requirements

In order to identify dynamics functions, it is fruitful to consider the functional requirements of the web application. These requirements contain assumptions on the behaviour of the web application, and it is these aspects that can be distilled into corresponding functional descriptions.

The functional requirements can be given in diverse formats, and there is no general rule that states how to identify and transform them into proper functions. Use cases, scenarios or user stories are valuable sources for finding functional requirements. The idea is to try and define indivisible functions that can be used to build more complex functions, which eventually capture all functional requirements that were initially identified. One should begin with writing down *signatures* of functions, and then define the desired semantics, possibly using natural language for the first stage, transforming it into a formal specification. Using the terminology as given by the content model and the query and update functions, the dynamics functions can be built in a straight-forward manner. Some dynamics functions might require new query or update functions, so these are added to the set of available functions as need may be.

7.2 Dynamics Functions for the Example Web Site

The Computer Science Faculty web site is a good example of a web site having almost *no* dynamic elements. There are no shopping baskets or user forums, and there is no necessity for session data, except for data used to store authentication information. In order to give an example for dynamics functions, we will therefore be a little bit more creative and present a possible application of dynamics functions that might be somewhat artificial, but it is perfectly reasonable nonetheless.

Let us assume that the search form for querying person information imposes the restriction that the length of the search string must not exceed 8 characters, and that it has to be converted to all lower case prior to using it in a query. The length restriction results from a corresponding load-reducing strategy for the web server, which was imposed after having tested a number of queries and the resulting response times. These times were almost optimal when the search strings had 8 characters or less, but did rise significantly for longer strings. The conversion to lower case is also due to constraints that are put forward by the search engine used.

These two restrictions are admittedly fictive, but may very well be experienced in real-world settings, so it makes sense, and not only for demonstration purposes, to define dynamics functions that exactly solve these problems.

The following function definition captures both restrictions by producing only valid search strings from any given string:

```
createValidSearchString :: String → String
createValidSearchString = (map Char.toLower) . (take 8)
```

The predefined function **take** extracts the first n elements of a given list. If the list is shorter than n, the whole list is returned. Since strings are lists, this function works fine in our context. In our definition for createValidSearchString, the resulting string is converted to all lower case by mapping the function **toLower** from the standard package **Char** over it.

The function just defined will be used in the page function that does the actual searching. Its description will be found on page 89.

Page Functions

Up to now, we have introduced the content model as the conceptualisation of the application domain, queries, and updates, which are accompanied with data types for an additional level of abstraction. Query and update functions operate on the instance data which is stored in a graph. The graph, in turn, complies to the content model. Yet another important building block are the dynamics functions that encapsulate the application's behaviour. Now, we are ready to put it all together.

Delivering a web site demands the production, and as a prerequisite, the definition, of single pages. They are at the heart of every web site. This chapter provides the necessary inventory to define what the pages are actually made of. *Page functions* will be used to compose pages, with recourse to queries and dynamics functions. The product of this composition will be an *abstract* representation of the final pages, as we will not consider any presentational details at this stage of modelling. The abstract representation will be introduced first, in section 8.1. After that, the page functions themselves will be explained in section 8.2, along with simple examples. Page functions offer many advantages, like additional levels of abstraction (see section 8.3), the possibility to access the system state (see section 8.4), the possibility to impose a template system on top of them (see section 8.5), and the possibility to do testing and simulation (see section 8.6). The chapter concludes by offering additional example page functions (section 8.7).

8.1 Abstract Page Descriptions

The result of calling a page function is an abstract description of the final page. It is abstract in the sense that it does not contain any information concerning the *presentation* of the page, but rather consists of a regular structure of elements that can be mapped to a concrete visualisation at a later time. In order to provide the necessary level of formality, a *data type* is introduced that precisely defines the syntax of these structures. In the domain of functional programming languages, this data type defines a set of valid terms, which consist of constructor applications that potentially reference the data type itself, thus forming a recursive, hierarchical term structure. Note that these terms can also be regarded as representing *trees*, with each constructor application as a node. If one of a constructor's arguments contains a sub-term of the said data type, then this constructor represents an inner node of the tree. Otherwise, i.e., when it only refers to values of any other type, it is a leaf. We will use both 'views' interchangeably, and we will also apply tree-specific terminology to talk about terms, by, for example, referring to *child nodes* in a given *term*.

We call the data type that defines the syntax of those trees of elements *abstract page description (APD)*. The function that corresponds to a page returns a term of this type.

```
data APD =
      Text String
    | Element Name Attrs ElementList
    | Link Name Attrs ElementList Identifier Params
    | Form Name Attrs ElementList Identifier Params
    | Field Name Attrs ElementList String
    | Empty

type ElementList = [APD]
```

There are six constructors for the APD type. An APD term can be a simple text node (Text); an element (Element) with a name, a list of attributes, and a list of child terms; a link or a form (Link and Form) with a name, a list of attributes, a list of child terms, the identifier of the destination page, and a list of parameters that should be passed to this page; a field in a form (Field) with a name, a list of attributes, a list of child terms, and a default field content; or it can simply be empty (Empty). The recursive structure is given by those constructors that accept values of type ElementList, because they are lists of APD terms. Thus, the APD data type represents n-ary trees, where all nodes, except those of type Text or Empty, are named and attributed.

Note again that we shift freely between viewing an APD as a term and as a tree. Consequently, we will regard the constructors as a means to *type* the nodes of the tree, or, respectively, the values they construct. In the following, the term structure shall be highlighted along the list of constructors. At first, however, here are the remaining type synonym declarations that have not yet been given. They will be referred to in the upcoming text:

```
type Name = String
type Attrs = [(String, String)]
type Params = Attrs
type Identifier = String
```

Now for the six constructors:

Text

Text nodes represent simple text strings. The inner structure of these texts is of no concern for the APD, so it is allowed to put anything inside a text node that should be treated as a meaningless sequence of characters. Further transformation steps that work *on* the APD can impose additional constraints on the text syntax, of course, for example by expecting XML documents or XML fragments.

Text nodes do never have any children.

Element

Element nodes are the most general nodes, serving as a container for child nodes and as a possibility to store a set of attributes. This set of *attributes* is a mapping from keys to values, both of type **String**. This allows for storing arbitrary data inside the node that can be interpreted during subsequent function calls. The mapping itself is stored in form of a list of tuples.

There is no particular semantics defined for element nodes; the interpretation is completely up to the functions that work on the APD term. Element nodes bear a name, however, that can be employed to differentiate element nodes. The name need not be unique throughout the tree. In the example structures that follow, we will use the name of an element to label it with a 'type' string; see also section 8.3 for further thoughts about this idea of typing. If one confined an APD term to containing Text and Element nodes only, one could compare it to an XML document; then, the name of an APD element node corresponds to the name of an XML element (terminological identity intended), which appears inside the start and end tag of that element. One can also think of an APD element's name as a distinguished attribute.

Link

Link nodes represent, as the name hopefully suggests, links. In the context of APDs, a link is the connection of the link node to a second APD, given by the name of the function that represents the destination APD, and the parameters that are to be passed to it.

The name of a link must be unique inside the APD term it appears in. This constraint is necessary in order to be able to identify the link at the time it shall be triggered. Triggering a link may also involve the transmission of parameters to the destination page. Further explanations of these semantical issues will be given below.

The differences between link nodes and element nodes are, as far as the APD syntax is concerned, of a minuscule degree. However, it was deliberately decided to include this distinguished notion of links into the APD definition because links are an important, not to say central, concept of hypertexts. Furthermore, all functions dealing with APD terms may now differentiate link nodes from the other nodes more easily.

Form

Form nodes are special links. For us, a form is a collection of fields that can be filled with values, which are sent along to the link destination as soon as the form link is activated, i.e., when the form is submitted. The Form and Link constructor's signatures are equivalent, because there is no reason to differentiate between forms and links on the syntax level. The only relevant constraint that is imposed on APD terms is that form nodes, and only them, may contain field nodes. In fact, links and forms are very similar, and both concepts will be discussed together in section 8.2.3.

Field

Field nodes represent parts inside a form where values can be entered. These field contents are transferred when the corresponding form is submitted, which means that the destination page function is called with the field values as its arguments. A field itself may be of arbitrary structural complexity, and may contain child nodes that further specify the field's composition. See below for further explanations and examples.

Empty

Empty nodes do not convey any particular information or meaning. They may be used to construct the empty tree, or term, that is of the type APD.

8.2 Page Function Definitions

While the APD data type defines the abstract structure of a page, we are still lacking a means to *produce* APD terms in response to a request for a particular page. It is the page functions that provide this feature. Thus, they play an important role in the concert of the web site models, as they define the composition of the pages.

This section will show how page functions can be defined, by stating the preliminary definitions, giving example applications for them, and finally illustrating further uses and implications.

8.2.1 The Page Function Type

The type PageFunc is the function type for pages. It defines a mapping of parameters to an APD structure. Parameters are pairs of keys and values.

type PageFunc = Params $\rightarrow$ APD

This type is used for every page definition. One extension will be necessary in order to properly deal with the system state. Section 8.4 will provide the description of this extension.

Links and form destinations are defined in terms of function identifiers. In this context, a function of the type Id2PageFunc maps identifiers to real page functions.

type Id2PageFunc = Identifier $\rightarrow$ PageFunc

This implies that links are represented by terms in an APD structure, attached with a reference to the page function they link to. This also allows for link consistency checks. More about links will be given in the following sections.

8.2.2 Basic Examples

Before showing page definitions for pages from the computer science faculty web site, we will focus on simpler examples that are better suited to convey the fundamental features of page functions. As soon as the templating mechanism has been introduced in section 8.5, the 'real' pages can be regarded as well.

Feeling the urge to follow something that might be called a tradition, we begin with a page function that produces a 'global greeting':

```
homepage :: PageFunc
homepage [] = Element "pageheading" [] [Text "Hello␣world!"]
```

This code fragment states that the homepage function is only defined for an empty parameter list, in which case it returns a single element node named pageheading with no attributes and containing the text node that bears the text 'Hello world!'. The returned APD term is constant, which makes the page a *static* one.

Static pages, in contrast to dynamic ones, always return the same content, regardless of the values passed to them as parameters. They do not contain calls to other functions that might deliver calculated and varying page fragments. Consequently, those pages are, by definition, a special case of pages with dynamic content. In practice, completely static pages are used very sparingly, because even the rather simple act of delivering a localised version of a page, according to the current settings given by the visitor, calls for having pages with dynamic content.

Pages with dynamic content require changing APD structures according to parameters passed in or according to queries the page depends on.

As an example,

```
greetingPage :: PageFunc
greetingPage [("name", name)] =
    Element "pageheading" []
      [ Text "Hello"
      , Element "paragraph" [] [Text name]
      ]
```

defines a simple page that expects a parameter named name and yields an APD structure that contains a heading "Hello" and a paragraph repeating the name that was passed as the parameter. Thus

```
greetingPage [("name", "Torsten")]
```

gives

```
Element "pageheading" [] [
    Text "Hello",
    Element "paragraph" [] [Text "Torsten"]]
```

Incorporating query results into pages is nothing more than calling the function that encapsulates the query. Examples that demonstrate the use of queries will be given in section 8.7.

8.2.3 Forms and Links

While explaining the APD constructors, it was already argued for treating links and forms in like manner. Both forms and links inside pages are means to interactively navigate through the web site. A form is used for the site visitor to enter data that is necessary to dynamically calculate page content. Submitting a form effectively calls a new page that makes use of the data provided via the form. A link, likewise, calls for a new page to be delivered. Therefore, it makes sense to handle links and forms uniformly. One can go as far as to say that links are 'invisible forms', i.e., forms whose data is pre-defined, and not editable by the visitor.

This section introduces forms first, because they are the more general concept. After that, links are described as a specialisation of forms.

Forms

Pages may contain forms that are used to query data from the visitor. Forms are submitted and the form data is passed to a receiving page function as its arguments. This way, values of parameters to pages can be directly influenced by the visitor. The receiving page function 'acts' on the parameters and produces an appropriate result.

In order to represent a form that is to be included in a page, an APD expression may contain form elements that include the identifier of the function that shall receive the submitted form data. A form is created using the Form constructor function. It consumes five parameters: the name of the form (a page may contain any number of forms, so it is important to be able to identify them unambiguously), a list of attributes, a list of child elements that constitute the actual content of the form (i.e., the input fields, embedded in an arbitrary APD structure), the name of the receiving function (any page) and parameters that are to passed to this receiving function. The receiving page is called the *form action page*.

The *input fields* are represented using Field nodes. Each field has a unique name (unique in the scope of the form, that is), a set of attributes, a list of child nodes, and a string that may be used to supply a default value for this form field. The attributes can be used to store any additional information that is necessary to further specify the field. If the field shall represent a list of values for the visitor to choose from, for example, these values can be attached to the node by the means of the attributes. It is also possible to give a fields are more complex structure, by supplying further nested Element or Field nodes, thus enabling, e.g., full XForms coverage ([BM04]). However, most of the field types normally used on HTML based web pages are representable without adding this level of complexity.

The following code shows a page with a very simple form:

```
nameEntryForm :: PageFunc
nameEntryForm [] =
  Form
    "nameEntry"
    []
    [ Text "Your␣name:"
    , Field "name" [] [] ""
    ]
    "greetingPage" []
```

One can see that the page consists of just the form element named nameEntry, which in turn comprises two further elements, a text label and the input field name. The input field comes without any attributes, without any child elements, and it has its default content set to the empty string.

The last component is the reference to the function greetingPage that is meant to receive the form data as soon as the form is completed by the visitor. In order to be able to do so, it must consume a parameter name as given by the field inside the form. This function's definition was given above (see page 87).

The following page function shows a slightly more elaborate example. It contains a form for searching the people database. The form comprises a single text field for the visitor to enter the search string. A full-text search is performed and the list of matching person records is returned. The search result is displayed on the same page, that is, the form calls itself upon submit. This makes sense because the page does not only contain the search form, but can also receive a parameter (the search text), perform the search, and display the result. This step is omitted when the parameter is empty, which happens when the page is called for the first time.

```
fb4People :: PageFunc
fb4People params =
  let
    searchtext = createValidSearchString $
        fromMaybe "" (lookup "searchtext" params)
  in
    fb4MainTemplate $ Element "slots" []
      [ Element "pagetitle" [] [Text "People␣List"]
      , Element "pageheading" [] [Text "People"]
      , Element "body" []
        [ (conditional
            (searchtext ≠ "")
            (fb4PersonList [("personIds", unwords $ getPersonIds searchtext)])
            Empty
          )
        , Form "personSearchForm" []
          [ Text "Search␣for:"
          , Field "searchtext" [("type", "text")] [] searchtext
          ]
          "fb4People" []
```

```
      ]
    ]
```

The function definition contains a call to the conditional function defined in section 8.3 in order to decide whether the search result is to be included. The decision is done with the string comparison of the searchtext argument and the empty string. Should the search text be non-empty, it is passed to the getPersonIds function that does the actual searching. It returns a list of PersonRecord data that match the query. This list is converted to an APD with the page function fb4PersonList that will be defined in section 8.7.2. Since it expects the identifiers separated by blanks in the parameter called personIds, this is performed by the **unwords** standard function. If the search text is empty, on the other hand, an Empty node is inserted instead.

The form inside the page uses as its action page the fb4SearchPage function it is defined in.

The getPersonIds function is a wrapper around the queryPersonIdsByName query function (see section 6.3):

```
getPersonIds :: String → [String]
getPersonIds = queryPersonIdsByName fb4
```

Note also that this functions uses the createValidSearchString dynamics function from section 7.2 to make sure that the search string is valid in respect to the length and case constraints imposed by the requirements stated in that section.

Links

A link inside a page is represented by a Link node in the corresponding APD structure. For example,

```
Link
  "homepageLink"
  []
  [Text "Back␣to␣the␣homepage"]
  "homepage" []
```

shows a link with the identifier homepageLink, no attributes, a text node inside describing the link, and an identifier of a function to be called when the link is activated by the visitor. As one can see, the structure of links is analogous to that of forms.

As far as the possible child elements of links are concerned, some restrictions apply. Links are not allowed to contain further links, nor forms or form fields. It only makes sense to put text nodes and element nodes inside the link and use them to describe the link (using element nodes to structure the text, as need may be).

The function supplied as the link destination can be any page. It is also possible to transport arguments to this page, or to specify the identifier of a virtual page (see section 8.2.4). These parameters are then simply added to the page function call. Note that the only difference to forms is the fact that the arguments have to be hard-coded into the page definition of the page containing the link, whereas arguments defined by form data can be supplied by the web site visitor and are received by the page containing the form (as soon as the form has been submitted).

Section 8.7 will provide more examples for links and forms. See also section 8.6 for information on triggering links and forms programmatically for purposes of simulation and testing.

8.2.4 Virtual Pages

A virtual page is a generic page that is computed *in its entirety* at run-time. In contrast to the other page types, virtual pages have no fixed identifier. Rather, this identifier is supplied as a parameter, so that the page can be created on-the-fly. The conceptual difference to normal pages is that the whole *page* depends on this parameter, and not only its contents. In other words, every possible value of the identifying parameter calls for one new, distinct, incarnation (instance) of that page. We will use the term *instance* to talk about concrete virtual pages. There is one instance for each possible identifier.

As an example, consider the faculty web site that shall provide a personal page for every staff member, showing data like the name and the person's phone number. These pages have a predefined structure, the only thing that changes from page to page is the data. Therefore, the page 'skeleton' is defined only once, by making it a virtual page. The name of the virtual page is Person(id), which signifies that the instances depend on one parameter, which in this case is the id of a given person.

To map this concept into the world of page functions, one can think of virtual pages as being represented by page functions with one additional parameter that contributes to the definition of their name. Therefore, we do not need to create a distinct function type for virtual pages. Rather, we state that a virtual page must be supplied with the parameter 'id' that has the page's identifier as its value. This is a mere convention, and adhering to it is completely in the obligation of the person or the software that produces the page function definitions.

8.3 Levels of Abstraction

Page functions are a powerful means to define the composition of web pages. First and foremost, they can utilise the full set of expressive power of the functional language they are written in. Any function is callable, be it provided by the language itself, by one of the accompanying or by external libraries, or be it specifically defined in the course of web site specification. This power enables a wealth of possible approaches for actually specifying the pages, which is the appropriate answer to the highly varying level of complexity of the concrete web applications that might be subject to specification. It is only this high level of flexibility that guarantees that one can choose exactly that level of abstraction that is asked for.

As far as the page functions are concerned, we see three possible ways to gain the appropriate levels of abstraction: adjusting the granularity of fragmentation for the composition of pages from fragments, using higher-level functions for the construction of APD terms, and defining the language that is represented by an APD term.

APD Language

We will begin by reconsidering the APD. It is abstract, and does not impose any prerequisite constraints on the output language the page is eventually transformed into. This leaves it open to the specification team to come up with a definition of the element types that should be used in the page functions for the construction of the APD terms. The reader will recall that all APD nodes, except text nodes and the empty node, have an identifier which can be any string. For nodes constructed by the Element constructor, this identifier should be the name of a type that is used in the process of transforming the APD into a concrete output language. The type might be, as an example, paragraph, which could be converted into the XHTML element named 'p'.

We suggest that there should be *one* set of element types that is consistently used for all pages; although it is possible to use, as an extreme case, a different APD for every page. It is the obligation of the presentation functions (which will be introduced in chapter 10) to map the APD into the output language of choice, and, here again, any amount of computational complexity can be employed to perform this transformation.

The set of element types that is agreed upon can be called a *language*, whose abstract syntax is given by the APD.

Higher-Level Functions

The logical structure of pages can be constructed by using helper functions. These functions each yield an APD structure. The application of those functions lifts the definitions to another level of abstraction. In the following, we will focus on functions that introduce a more convenient and powerful way to express *control flow*. At this point, one can again see the benefits of the functional approach, as the ideas presented here are just examples of what is realisable in principle. Building *upon* these definitions is always possible and allows moving on step by step, as far as is appropriate and helpful.

The first function can be used to include or omit content based on conditions. It is a wrapper around **if**..**then**..**else** expressions, using the appropriate types.

```
conditional :: Bool → APD → APD → APD
conditional b t f = if b then t else f
```

As an example, regard

```
loginAction :: PageFunc
loginAction [("login", v1)] =
    conditional
        ( v1 == "charlie" )
        (Text "Hello␣Charlie!␣Hope␣you␣enjoyed␣your␣holiday!")
        (Text (v1 ++ "␣logged␣in"))
```

which presents an individualised message if the user name equals to charlie.

The second function can be used to iterate over a list, producing APD terms for each list element and collecting these terms inside a given outer element. The function expects three parameters: a list with elements of any type a, one APD structure that must be an Element with no children, and a function that maps objects of type a to APD structures.

```
foreach :: [a] → APD → (a → APD) → APD
```

The function can be defined as follows:

```
foreach items (Element cname cattr []) itemMap =
    Element cname cattr (map itemMap items)
```

The given Element itself is returned unchanged. However, it receives a list of child elements that is constructed by applying the given function to each element of the list.

The following example page uses such a loop:

```
p1 :: APD
p1 = foreach [1,2,3]
    (Element "tr" [] [])
    (λm → (Element "td" [] [Text (show m)]))
```

The page consists of an iteration over the list [1, 2, 3], which could be the result of a query call. For each element in that list, the Element tr is used as a container for the list of 'td's. The third parameter to foreach is a lambda expression that maps each number to a td element that contains the integer value as a text. The show function converts a number into a string using decimal notation.

The expression p1 evaluates to

```
Element "tr" []
    [Element "td" [] [Text "1"],
    Element "td" [] [Text "2"],
    Element "td" [] [Text "3"]
    ]
```

Page Fragments

Functions that describe page fragments demonstrate another benefit gained from using a programming language to describe abstract pages. Complex APD structures can be assembled from a set of simpler functions that each describe a well-defined part of a page (divide et impera). Each part, in turn, can employ any feature offered by the programming language, giving them great expressive power. Clearly, this approach also fosters re-use of page fragments, and a site designer tends to devise functions in a way that allows them to be used in as many contexts as possible.

Yet another means to build pages from parts are *page templates* that help to define an outer frame for pages that can be filled at pre-defined places. Please confer section 8.5 for further details.

8.4 On State

Page functions are allowed to depend on any kind of context information, including the state of the system. They may also change the system state, either indirectly by calling dynamics functions that apply changes to the instance data, or directly by performing these changes themselves. The notion of 'state' is a somewhat foreign concept in a functional world, as was already pointed out in section 3.3, but by employing monads it is possible to handle statefulness conveniently.

In our case, we treat 'state' as a value that is threaded through each function call, very much like an implicit parameter. The functions may also change the state, which results in the updated value being passed on to the next function. The predefined StateT monad is used to abstract from this state-passing semantics.

We regard the term *context information* as being very broad, subsuming the notion of state. The context information comprises the current instance data, that is, the instance graph, as well as *session data*. Session data is any data that is available for the current session *apart* from the information stored in the graph. This comprises authentication information, temporary data like shopping basket contents, as well as any data passed in from the outside, like the web site visitor's current geographic position, the output device, or localisation-relevant data. All session data is stored in a key/value-based dictionary of type SessionData, and is jointly packed together with the instance graph to form a tuple that represents the current context information:

```
type SessionData = AttributedLabel
type SessionContext = (AttributedGraph, SessionData)
```

The type AttributedLabel was defined in section 3.4.2, it represents a dictionary.

In order to nudge the context information around, it is packed into a monadic type that combines an IO monad and a state monad:

```
type Stateful a = StateT SessionContext IO a
```

This type effectively passes a value of type SessionContext along every I/O operation. The computation of the final state starts with a concrete session context tuple and eventually returns a result of type a. This construct allows for the definition of state-aware page functions:

```
type StatefulAPD = Stateful APD
type StatefulPageFunc = Params → StatefulAPD
```

A page function of this kind receives parameters, as usual, but it does not directly return an APD. Rather, it returns a StateT value that encapsulates a *computation* which describes the transformation of a given, initial state to the final APD. In order to actually produce a result, this computation must be evaluated, which can be achieved by using the function runStateT from the module that also contains the definition for the StateT monad. This function takes one StateT value and one SessionContext value and produces a tuple: the final SessionContext value, along with the APD term that was returned by the page function.

Let us look at a simple example:

```
example :: StatefulPageFunc
example p = do
   (g,s) ← get
   put (insNode (99, NoAttributes) g, setValue s "id" "someID")
   return (Element "main" [] [])
```

This page function reads the current state and binds it to the tuple (g,s). It changes the state via the put operation by inserting a new node with number 99 into the graph g, and assigning a value to a key in s. Finally, it returns one APD element.

Running this page function involves the evaluation of:

```
exampletest = runStateT
   (example [])                                                    (1)
   (mkGraph [] [], NoAttributes)                                   (2)
```

The page function itself is called with an empty parameter list (see mark (1)), and the initial context information tuple consists of an empty graph and an empty session dictionary (see mark (2)). The value of exampletest is

```
( Element "main" [] []
, ( 99:−>[], {id:=someID} )
)
```

This is a tuple, whose first element is the APD, and the second is another tuple consisting of the graph (we see the node number 99 with an empty list of outgoing edges) and the session dictionary that contains the value someID for the key id.

8.5 Page Templates

8.5.1 Motivation

Many, if not all, web pages in a web site share a common design and there are many elements that are required to appear on more than one page. When designing a web site, these elements should be identified and one or more generic and schematic pages should be set up that serve as *templates* for other pages.

When using functions for defining web pages, as we do in this text, this kind of template mechanism can quite easily be implemented with functions as well. Conceptually, a template is a page with a given set of named *slots*. These slots are compartments that can be filled with the actual content when applying the template to a concrete page. In the template definition, the slots are embedded in a complete page that contains, besides the slots, all the common elements that are to appear on every page that uses the template.

Technically, the template is defined to be a function that not only yields an APD, but that also receives an APD as input. The function transforms this APD into the destination page. The input APD contains definitions about *what* to put into the slots provided by the template, and the template function defines *where* to put the slot contents on the page.

Apart from being the most coherent way to defining the templates, using a function to do so also offers the additional benefit of being able to create 'sophisticated' templates that *process* the content that is put into the slots. Thus, the template may involve more than just a simple mapping from content to slot. It can contain conditional expressions that, for example, put the content at different places depending on the content itself or depending on external conditions, or change the content before putting it into the resulting page. The template, in the end, can call *any* other function which also makes it possible to partition complex templates into more convenient fragments and to re-use these fragments for multiple templates. It might even be appropriate to use nested templates, i.e., templates that call other templates.

Templates need not necessarily result in complete pages, but can of course be equally used to produce page *fragments*. Thus, it is possible to define templates for specific non-trivial, recurring parts that shall be structured consistently on several pages throughout the web site. A simplistic example might be the treatment of photos: consider that one might demand that photos should always have a caption that is to be displayed along with the photo itself. A simple template with two slots, one for the photo and one for the caption, could then be used in page functions to format photos in a consistent way. The page functions using this template only provide the two required slot contents, and the template function then takes care to produce the actual APD, which may be arbitrarily complex, depending on the chosen abstract language.

For the Computer Science Faculty web site, one single template is used that defines the general structure for all of the pages. Before showing this template, the following part of this section formally defines the template mechanism.

8.5.2 Definition of the Template Functions

A template function is a function $f : \text{APD} \rightarrow \text{APD}$. This signature emphasises that it is a *filter* that can be interposed in the transformation process (in the sense of a pipe/filter architecture). The function transforms one APD term into another. In principle, there are no constraints as to which transformations are performed, as long as the processing of the slots is done in accordance to the following definitions.

The input APD that is provided by the page function that *calls* the template must obey some simple rules concerning its structure:

- The root element must be named slots. In other words: the APD term must be an Element value with its name, which is the first parameter of the Element constructor, set to the string 'slots'. When regarding the term as a tree, this is equivalent to the root node.

- The root element may contain zero or more child elements (*slot content elements*) whose names correspond to slot identifiers as defined by the template. A slot content element comprises, as child nodes, the actual slot contents, which may be arbitrary APD terms.

- Slot content elements *only* appear as direct children of the root (slot) element.

The template function embeds slot contents into the page it defines. In order to do so, it searches for slot content elements of a given name by iterating over the children of the root element.

The template function may provide *default slot contents* for any of the slots. When the input APD contains no slot content element with the identifier defined in the template, the slot in question may be filled with content provided by the template function. As a consequence, the caller can regard the template function as merely offering *possibilities* to overwrite certain parts of the template page.

For a template function to become useful, it should be accompanied by an interface definition that describes the template, i.e., the slots and the immutable parts. The description should include a listing of the available slots (i.e., the slot identifiers), their intended use and their default contents, if available. The interface definition should also include a pictorial diagram like the one in figure 8.1 showing where the slots are positioned on the final page and which common parts will be included on every page. Note that the page template does not prescribe the final *presentation* of a page, and that the diagram is only a hint towards the suggested positioning.

8.5.3 Page Template Application Example

In the following, we shall apply the definitions given above to the Computer Science Faculty web site. We shall also introduce additional functions that have proven helpful in practice and that may be used in the actual template definition.

The template function fb4MainTemplate, whose code will be given below, provides the required mapping from APD to APD. The available slots are

- pagetitle – The title of the page as it appears in the HTML header.

- pageheading – The main heading of the page. The contents of this slot will be put at the top of the page.

- rightcolumn – A sidebar on the right hand side of the page.

- body – The main content of the page.

Figure 8.1 shows the position of the slots on the page, using the homepage as an example. Thus, the contents visible inside the slots are not the default contents provided by the template, but rather those supplied by the homepage (see section 8.7.1). Note that the

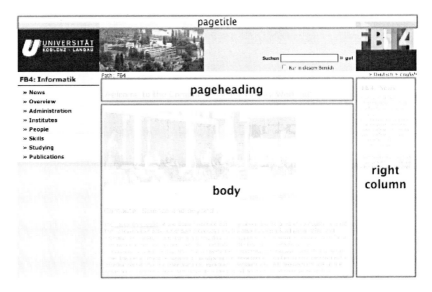

Figure 8.1: Main page template for the Computer Science Faculty Homepage

slot pagetitle is defined to be in the HTML header, so it has no visual representation on the page.

The function fb4MainTemplate is called with a slots element as parameter that contains the slot contents elements. The slots element is replaced with the template page, which basically consists of a table with three columns. The left column contains a navigation tree reflecting the primary navigation structure, the centre column contains the main page body, and the right column contains a sidebar that can be filled with additional topics that should be visually highlighted (e.g., news items).

For each slot, the template function filters those elements that have the specific slot identifier (there should be only one for each slot), and inserts the specified content at the designated places.

```
fb4MainTemplate :: APD → APD
fb4MainTemplate (Element "slots" a es) =
  Element "html" a
    [ Element "head" [] -- HTML head
      ( -- pagetitle slot
        if (length pagetitleContent) ≠ 0 then
          pagetitleContent
        else
          ( (++)
            (
              if (length pageheadingContent) ≠ 0 then
                ( (++)
```

```
                    (foldl (++) [] (map extractTextNodes pageheadingContent))
                    [Text "␣−␣"]
                )
              else
                []
            )
            [Text "Computer␣Science␣Faculty"]
          )
        )
    , Element "body" [] [ −− HTML body
      Element "table" [("border","1")]                                    (1)
      [ Element "tr" []
          [ Element "td" [("colspan","3")] [Text "Header"] −−− todo: header
          ]
      , Element "tr" []
        [ Element "td" []
            [ Link "home" [] [Text "Go␣Home"] "fb4Homepage" []
            , Element "br" [] []
            , Text "Navigation"
            ] −−− todo: navigation tree
        , Element "td" []  −− main body area
          ( ( −− pageheading slot
            if (length pageheadingContent) ≠ 0 then
              pageheadingContent
            else
              if (length pagetitleContent) ≠ 0 then
                pagetitleContent
              else
                []
          ) ++
          ( −− body slot                                                  (2)
            if (length bodyContent) ≠ 0 then
              bodyContent
            else
              [Text "Body−Slot"]
          ) )
        , Element "td" [("valign","top")] −− right column slot
          ( rightcolumnContent
          )
        ]
      , Element "tr" []
          [ Element "td" [("colspan","3")] [Text "Footer"] −−− todo: footer
          ]
      ]
    ]
]
where
  bodyContent = extractSlotContents "body" es                             (3)
  pageheadingContent = extractSlotContents"pageheading" es
```

```
    pagetitleContent = extractSlotContents "pagetitle" es
    rightcolumnContent = extractSlotContents "rightcolumn" es
```

As an example, let us look at the body slot. The slot is defined to be inside the main table, in the centre column. Starting from line (1), the template function creates one table element for the main table, and the body slot is contained in the second row (tr) in the second column (td). It is inserted by the lines following mark (2).

The variable bodyContent refers to the contents of the body slot. It is defined in the **where** clause (see mark (3)), where es is bound to the list of child elements of the slots element, i.e., the list of slot contents elements. The function extractSlotContents is used to extract the contents of the body slot from the input APD:

```
extractSlotContents :: String → [APD] → [APD]
extractSlotContents n es = foldr
    ((++).extractChildElements)
    []
    (filter (isElementWithName n) es)
```

The function takes the name of the desired slot and the list of slot elements as input, and returns the complete list of all matching child elements (there may be more than one element with a given slot name). The application of the **filter** function to this list results in the selection of the element with the name of the slot ('body', in our example), which contains the contents for the body slot (there *should* be only one, but the template function works flawlessly with an arbitrary list of body slot definitions). The resulting slot contents are packed together in a list. The function extractChildElements is used to strip off the enclosing slot element:

```
extractChildElements :: APD → [APD]
extractChildElements (Element e a es) = es
extractChildElements (Link e a es i p) = es
extractChildElements (Form e a es i p) = es
extractChildElements (Field e a es s) = es
extractChildElements _ = []
```

The following lines

```
( -- body slot
  if (length bodyContent) ≠ 0 then
      bodyContent
  else
    [Text "Body−Slot"]
)
```

then define the necessary mapping to insert the body slot contents into the final page. If bodyContent is not empty, the content is inserted. When there is no definition for the body slot in the calling function, a default slot content is produced that consists of a simple text element. One could also have defined an error condition here, because a page without a body does not make much sense. However, supplying this kind of 'dummy' content allows to produce preliminary draft pages that work despite of being incomplete and that can be filled at a later time.

The page template generates an APD structure. The element names used in the example are almost entirely borrowed from the HTML, which allows us to produce an HTML representation of the page by simply serialising the APD as XML. However, using HTML as the 'concrete language' to define the pages is not the preferred solution in the general case, because it predetermines the output language and one looses one layer of abstraction, as was already pointed out in section 8.3. In our special case, where the intent is to demonstrate the ideas, referring to HTML is beneficial because it is sufficiently suggestive without demanding for the definition of an additional abstraction level that would only obscure the examples and make it harder for the reader to follow.

8.6 Visitor Simulation and Page Function Testing

Page functions can be tested like any other kinds of functions. One defines the desired result for a given argument list, evaluates the function with these arguments, and compares the actual result to the anticipated one. This procedure is applicable to page functions as well, and one can test whether the resulting APD term corresponds to the structure that was intended to be produced for concrete given arguments and for a given system state, if the function happens to rely on it.

Taking into account that pages may contain links and forms, one realises that it is also possible to test-drive *successions* of pages by *simulating* the activation of links or forms. Consider a page p_1 that submits a form to page p_2. Instead of manually constructing a fixed set of arguments for the page p_2 in order to test it, one simply pretends that the user entered a certain set of values into the form on page p_1 and lets the system perform the call of the form action page p_2. The identifier of that page is contained in the form definition, along with additional parameters that should be sent along, and using an Id2PageFunc mapping (see section 8.2), the corresponding page function can be found and evaluated automatically. Note that this is a different type of test: simulating a form submission verifies that the destination page works as expected for a given set of form values. The submission is done automatically, analogously to the way it happened via HTTP. One can also test the form action page *in isolation*, by predefining the input parameters.

The same arguments hold for links as well, but we shall consider forms first. In the following, we show how the data can be transported to a form action page, and we will introduce a function that 'executes' a form and thus triggers the corresponding action.

Forms

The idea is to simulate a web site visitor who submits the form with a given set of input data. To support this, the following execForm function calls the specified form action page whose identifier appears in the form node given as second parameter.

```
execForm :: Id2PageFunc → APD → Params → APD
execForm ipf (Form n a es pid pa) params =
  ((ipf pid) (mergeParams pa params))
```

In order to determine which page function to call, the first parameter of type Id2PageFunc defines the mapping from the function identifier in the form node to the actual function. The third parameter to execForm is the form input data that is handed over to the form action page. This data is merged with the parameter list present in the form node in such a way that parameters passed to execForm overwrite parameters of the same name in the form node.

The function mergeParams, which performs the actual merging of two parameter lists, is defined as:

```
mergeParams :: Params → Params → Params
mergeParams a b =
  b ++ (filter (takeIfNotInList b) a)
  where
    takeIfNotInList :: Params → (String, String) → Bool
    takeIfNotInList ((ak,av):as) (k,v)
      | ak == k  = False
      | otherwise = takeIfNotInList as (k,v)
    takeIfNotInList _ _ = True
```

The function execForm is only defined for form nodes, and it is an error to pass along other kinds of nodes.

In order to find a particular form node inside a page, the following findForm function can be used. It accepts as parameters an APD term containing the form, and an identifier for the form (the APD structure might contain more than one form). The function returns the form node specified by the second parameter, or Empty in the case that no form of this name can be found.

```
findForm :: APD → String → APD
findForm (Text s) _ = Empty
findForm (Element n a []) _ = Empty
findForm (Element n a (e:es)) formId =
  let firstElement = findForm e formId
  in
    if isEmpty firstElement
    then findForm (Element n a es) formId
    else firstElement
findForm (Link n a e pid pa) linkId  = Empty
findForm form@(Form n a e pid pa) formId
  | n == formId   = form
  | otherwise     = Empty
findForm (Field n a es s) _ = Empty
findForm Empty _ = Empty
```

The patterns in the function definition directly reflect the APD definition. The given APD structure is traversed in a recursive manner. A text node, a field node, and the empty APD structure can be ignored, and an Empty value is returned in all three cases. A link node is ignored as well, because it is not allowed to include forms inside links.

An element node (Element) may contain a list of child nodes. Therefore, findForm is called recursively for each child node as long as those calls return Empty. The result of the first call that yields a non-empty APD structure is returned, because this must be the form node searched for.

If the first element in the list of child elements yields Empty when passed to findForm, the tail of this list must be checked analogously. To do so, findForm is called recursively on a newly created element node that contains all remaining child elements, i.e., the original list of child elements, minus the head that just proved to deliver Empty. It is ok to create this kind of wrapper element around the list because the element itself is not considered in the recursive calls that follow. It is only the child elements that count.

In order to compare a node to the Empty node, we use a function isEmpty, defined as follows:

```
isEmpty :: APD → Bool
isEmpty Empty = True
isEmpty _ = False
```

This simple function employs pattern matching to check whether a given APD element is the Empty element, returning **True** in this case. In all other cases, **False** is returned.

The last case in the definition of findForm deals with form elements in the given APD structure:

```
findForm form@(Form n a e pid pa) formId
  | n == formId  = form
  | otherwise    = Empty
```

The definition uses a case pattern to filter out the form node specified by the given form identifier (the last parameter, bound by formId). If the current form actually is the one asked for, i.e., if n equals formId, the form node that matched the pattern is returned. Otherwise, an Empty node is returned.

The following code shows how to supply actual parameters to a form. Consider the following form page containing two forms:

```
multiForm :: PageFunc
multiForm [] =
  Element "p" [] [
    Form
      "form1"
      []
      [Field "searchText" [] [] "default"]
      "searchAction" [],
    Form
```

```
      "form2"
      []
      [Field "name" [] [] "",
       Link "home" [] [Text "Help"] "homepage" []
      ]
      "greetingPage" []
  ]
```

We can test the second form by evaluating

```
multiformtest =
    (execForm
          pageFuncFromPageId
          (findForm (multiForm []) "form2")
          [("name", "Alice")]
    )
```

This call executes form number two of the multiForm page and pretends that the web site visitor has entered the string "Alice" in the name form field. One can see that findForm is used to retrieve the form node from the APD structure, and execForm is called on the result node, passing the form data as parameter. The function pageFuncFromPageId, that is passed to execForm as first parameter, is the mapping function that maps function identifiers to actual functions. The relevant pattern in its definition is:

```
pageFuncFromPageId :: Id2PageFunc
...
pageFuncFromPageId "greetingPage" = greetingPage
...
```

The page function greetingPage was presented on page 87.

When run in Haskell, the program yields:

```
Element "pageheading" [] ["Hello",Element "paragraph" [] ["Alice"]]
```

Links

In order to be able to execute a *link* and go on with the page thus called for, we can proceed analogously to forms: the function execLink triggers the function that was attached to the link node via the function identifier. The execLink function is called with three parameters: an Id2PageFunc mapping from identifiers to functions, an APD structure, which must be a link node, and a set of attribute/value pairs that are to be passed to the function that returns the target page.

```
execLink :: Id2PageFunc → APD → Params → APD
execLink ipf (Link n a e pid pa) params =
    ((ipf pid) (mergeParams pa params))
```

The following function provides a way to find the link in question inside a given APD structure and to return the node containing the link definition. Since a page may contain any number of links, an identifier has to be supplied that specifies which link shall be found.

```
findLink :: APD → String → APD
findLink (Text s) _ = Empty
findLink (Element n a []) _ = Empty
findLink (Element n a (e:es)) linkId =
    let firstElement = findLink e linkId
    in
        if isEmpty firstElement
        then findLink (Element n a es) linkId
        else firstElement
findLink link@(Link n a e pid pa) linkId
    | n == linkId    = link
    | otherwise      = Empty
findLink (Form n a [] pid pa) _ = Empty
findLink (Form n a (e:es) pid pa) linkId =
    let firstElement = findLink e linkId
    in
        if isEmpty firstElement
        then findLink (Form n a es pid pa) linkId
        else firstElement
findLink (Field n a es s) linkId =
    -- search through es recursively
    head $
    ( filter (not . isEmpty) $ map (λa → findLink a linkId) es )
    ++ [Empty]        -- safety belt for 'head'
findLink Empty _ = Empty
```

Apparently, the function findLink works almost analogously to findForm, so the reader can be referred to the explanations above. The only differences are the pattern concerning the Link element, which is where the link node is returned when the link identifier equals the identifier supplied as parameter, and the two patterns for the Form element. Like element nodes, form nodes are searched for link nodes among their children by recursively calling findLink until the first non-empty node is returned, which signifies that the correct link node was found.

To close the example, the last code snippet contains an application of the search form with an actual search and a simulation of following a link on the result page. Evaluating

```
peopleSearchPageTest =
    (execLink
        pageFuncFromPageId
        (findLink
            (execForm
                pageFuncFromPageId
                (findForm
                    (fb4People [("searchtext", "")])
                    "peopleSearchForm"
```

```
            )
              [("searchtext", "Alice")]
            )
            "personHomepage/alice"
          )
        []
    )
```

performs the following steps: First, the search page peopleSearchPage (cf. its definition on page 89) is called with an empty search string. Then, execForm is called on the result of findForm, and the form named peopleSearchForm (which is the name of the only form on this page) is filled with the search text. The execForm function executes the form, which means that it returns the form action page (which, in our case, is the search form itself). This page now contains the search result, namely the table with the (one and only) corresponding person data. Inside the table, there is a link to the homepage of the person. This link is then triggered using the execLink function, which is supplied with the name of the link to be activated (personHomepage/alice) and an empty argument list.

The evaluation of peopleSearchPageTest yields

```
Element "page" []
  [Element "h1" [] ["alice"],Element "p" [] ["Id:␣alice"]]
```

which is the homepage of the person searched for.

8.7 Page Functions for the Example Web Site

This section deals with the functional descriptions of the pages that constitute the Computer Science Faculty web site. So far, a number of example page functions have already been given throughout this chapter, but the following functions are more realistic in the sense that they can actually be used for the Computer Science Faculty web site. Among these functions are also those that do not return a whole page, but rather just page fragments.

The page functions make use of the *page template function* introduced in section 8.5, that makes it more convenient to define the set of page parts that are common to every page. The functions also rely on several supplementary functions that deal with querying data or with the conversion of types, which were already presented in section 6.3.

8.7.1 Homepage

The home page (Homepage) is the entry point into the site and is set up to welcome the visitor. The page is designed around a current photo that is changed every few weeks. Next to the photo, which is produced by the function fb4CurrentPhoto (section 8.7.7), there is a listing of the most current news items as well as an introductory text with links to important pages for selected visitor groups. Like for all pages, the navigation menu is displayed on the left side of the page to let the visitor choose from the set of pages that are one level below the top-level.

The news item list is generated by calling the corresponding function fb4CurrentNews (section 8.7.5). It returns, for a given list of category items, a list with the most current news entries that belong to at least one of the given categories. Each news item can be categorised by attaching a list of strings to it. These strings are then used for filtering. Below the list, there is a link to the News page (fb4News (section 8.7.3)).

The introductory text on the homepage is a page fragment in its own right, produced by the function fb4HomepageIntroductoryText (section 8.7.8). This is necessary because the text is not a static item, but has to be calculated according to the current language settings: when the site visitor chooses a different language, which is possible on every web page in the site by clicking the corresponding link in the page heading, every translatable item has to be delivered in the correct localisation. The web site is set up in a way so that each item (i.e., texts and images) is presented using the current language. If the corresponding version of the item for the preferred language is not available, a default version is automatically selected and delivered instead. This compromise was chosen intentionally: this algorithm will result in pages with mixed languages when some parts are translated appropriately, and others are not. But this situation was valued less severe than omitting text fragments altogether, which might lead to even more confusion. Note that that the language switching mechanism is omitted from the example specifications.

```
fb4Homepage :: PageFunc
fb4Homepage [] = fb4MainTemplate
  (Element "slots" []
    [ Element "pagetitle" [] [Text "Faculty␣Homepage"]
    , Element "pageheading" [] [Text "Welcome"]
    , Element "rightcolumn" []
      [ Element "div" [("class","rightColumnHeadline")] [Text "FB4␣−␣News"]
        , (fb4CurrentNews
            [("categoryList", "FB4"), ("maxcount","5")])
        , Link "newsitemListLink" [] [Text "All␣the␣news"]
          "fb4News" []
      ]
    , Element "body" [] [
        (fb4CurrentPhoto []),
        (fb4HomepageIntroductoryText [])
      ]
    ]
  ])
```

Figure 8.2 shows the rendered version of the HTML code generated by the fb4Homepage function as defined above.

8.7.2 PersonList

The PersonList page is given by:

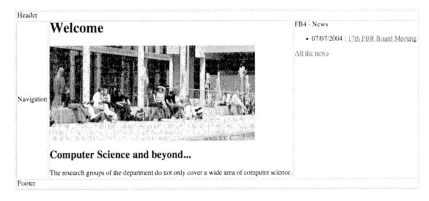

Figure 8.2: Generated Computer Science Faculty Homepage

```
fb4PersonList :: PageFunc
fb4PersonList params =
  let
    personIds = words $ fromJust $ lookup "personIds" params
    personList = (map (fromJust . getPersonById) personIds)
  in
    foreach
      personList
      (Element "table" [("class","personTable")] [])
      (λ p →
        Element "tr" []
          [ Element "td" []
              [ Link
                  ("personHomepage/" ++ (personId p))
                  []
                  [Text $ personId p ]
                  "personHomepage" [("id", (personId p))]
              ]
          , Element "td" [] [ Text $ name p ]
          , Element "td" [] [ Element "a" [("href", url p)] [Text $ url p] ]
          ]
      )
```

This page fragment consists of a table with one row (tr) for each person. The table has two columns (td), one displaying the name of the person, the other containing a link to person's homepage. The link elements are supplied with identifiers by concatenating the string 'personHomepage/' with the identifier of a person. This is necessary because every link on a page must have a unique identifier[1].

---

[1] Two links on one page may have the same identifier if they call the same function with the same arguments upon activation.

The expressions name p, personId p, and url p refer to the selector functions declared in the PersonRecord data type (see section 6.2). Since p is of the type PersonRecord, the three functions can be applied to p and return the corresponding data element.

The links inside the peopleList page fragment are destined to lead to a virtual page named personHomepage. One can see that the identifier of the person is coded into the link definition. The target page function might look like this:

```
personHomepage :: PageFunc
personHomepage [("id", personId)] =
  Element "page" [] [
    Element "h1" [] [Text personId],
    Element "p" [] [Text ("Id:␣" ++ personId)]
  ]
```

The page consists of a heading and a simple text node that repeats the identifier passed in.

8.7.3 News

The News page presents an introductory text (fb4NewsIntroductoryText (section 8.7.9)) and a news listing (fb4CurrentNewsTable (section 8.7.6)). The news listing on the News page appears in the body area, and not in the right sidebar, as it does on the homepage. This flexibility is a side-effect from using functions like fb4CurrentNews/fb4CurrentNewsTable that produce coherent page fragments.

```
fb4News :: PageFunc
fb4News [] = fb4MainTemplate
  (Element "slots" []
    [ Element "pagetitle" [] [Text "News"]
    , Element "pageheading" [] [Text "News"]
    , Element "body" [] [
        (fb4NewsIntroductoryText []),
        (fb4CurrentNewsTable [("categoryList", "FB4")])
      ]
    ])
```

8.7.4 NewsItem

The NewsItem page is a virtual page that shows information on one particular news item. The identifier of the news item is passed in as parameter.

The code printed below shows how to deal with errors that may occur when composing a page. In this case, it might happen that the identifier supplied as parameter is not a legal one, i.e., that there exists no news item with this specific identifier.

The NewsItem page shows an error message if the requested news item cannot be found. Otherwise, the news item's title and the description are printed.

```
fb4NewsItem :: PageFunc
fb4NewsItem [("id", newsid)] = fb4MainTemplate
  (Element "slots" []
    [ Element "pagetitle" [] [Text "News"]
    , Element "pageheading" [] [Text "News"]
    , Element "body" []
      (let
          news = getNewsById newsid
       in
          if (isNothing news) then
            [(fb4ErrorMessage [
              ("title", "Error"),
              ("description", newsid++"␣does␣not␣exist.")
            ])]
          else
            (let
                (date, shortTitle, shortDesc, newsid) =
                  fromJust news
             in
                [ Element "heading" [] [Text shortTitle]
                , Element "p" [] [Text shortDesc]
                ]
            )
      )
  ])
```

8.7.5 CurrentNews

The CurrentNews page fragment produces a list with news items. The set of news items to be displayed is defined by the parameters to this function, which are passed on to getCurrentNews (section 8.7.11).

```
-- Converts a news item list to an HTML enumeration
fb4CurrentNews :: PageFunc
fb4CurrentNews params =
    foreach
      (getCurrentNews params)
      (Element "ul" [("class","newsitemList")] [])
      (λ(date, shortTitle, shortDesc, newsid) →
        Element "li" [("class","newsitem")]
          [ Element "span" [("class","newsitemDate")] [Text date]
          , Text ":"
          , Link "newsitemLink" [] [Text shortTitle]
              "fb4NewsItem" [("id", newsid)]
          ]
      )
```

8.7.6 CurrentNewsTable

The CurrentNewsTable page fragments works exactly like fb4CurrentNews (section 8.7.5), except that it displays news items as a table and not as an enumeration.

```
—— Converts a news item list to an HTML table
fb4CurrentNewsTable :: PageFunc
fb4CurrentNewsTable params =
   foreach
      (getCurrentNews params)
      (Element "table" [("class","newsitemTable")] [])
      (λ(date, shortTitle, shortDesc, newsid) →
          Element "tr" [("class","newsitem")]
          [ Element "td" [] [Text date]
          , Element "td" []
            [ Link ("newsitemLink" ++ newsid) [] [Text shortTitle]
               "fb4NewsItem" [("id", newsid)]
            ]
          , Element "td" [] [Text shortDesc]
          ]
      )
```

8.7.7 CurrentPhoto

The fb4CurrentPhoto page function returns an element that references the 'photo of the week.' It utilises a function resourceURL to generate a URL to the photo.

```
fb4CurrentPhoto :: PageFunc
fb4CurrentPhoto [] =
   Element "img"
      [ ("src", (resourceURL "currentPhoto"))
      , ("alt", "Photo␣of␣the␣week")—— should  be property of the photo
      ]
      []
```

8.7.8 HomepageIntroductoryText

The following function returns an introductory text to be put on the homepage.

```
fb4HomepageIntroductoryText :: PageFunc
fb4HomepageIntroductoryText [] =
   Element "div" []
      [ Element "h2" []
          [Text "Computer␣Science␣and␣beyond..."]
      , Text "The␣"
      , Text "research␣groups"
      , Text "␣of␣the␣department␣do␣not␣only␣cover␣a␣wide␣area␣of␣computer␣science."
```

```
      ]
```

8.7.9 NewsIntroductoryText

The fb4NewsIntroductoryText function returns an introductory text to be put before the listing of the most current news items on the News page.

```
fb4NewsIntroductoryText :: PageFunc
fb4NewsIntroductoryText [] =
  Element "div" []
    [ Element "h2" [] [Text "Top␣News"]
    , Text "Here␣you␣see␣the␣most␣current␣news␣items."
    ]
```

8.7.10 ErrorMessage

Producing a page fragment with an error message is achieved with the following function. A title (e.g., 'Error', 'Warning') and a description can be supplied as parameters.

```
fb4ErrorMessage :: PageFunc
fb4ErrorMessage params =
  let
    title = fromJust (lookup "title" params)
    description = fromJust (lookup "description" params)
  in
    (Element "Empty" []
      [ Element "heading" [] [ Text title ]
      , Element "p" [] [ Text description ]
      ]
    )
```

8.7.11 Supplementary Functions

The page functions defined above make use of supplementary functions that provide an additional abstraction layer on top of the query functions. We will only give the code for one of the functions, as they are sufficiently simple and alike.

getPersonById

The following function is a wrapper around the queryPersonById query function, defined in section 6.3.2.

```
getPersonById :: String → Maybe PersonRecord
getPersonById = queryPersonById fb4
```

The identifier fb4 references the instance graph.

getCurrentNews

Returns a list of current news items.

getNewsById

Returns the news item identified by the given **String** argument. If there is no such news item, the **lookup** function will return **Nothing**.

Navigation Structure

While the page functions describe the single pages of the web site, the interconnection of the pages via links is to be taken care of as well. The navigation structure does exactly this. In this context, we will also consider issues related to authorisation, because parts of the web site might be intended to be accessible for authorised visitors only.

This chapter will provide a visual notation that allows to depict the structure that results from the hyperlinks between pages. We differentiate these links into two categories: *primary* links constitute a strict hierarchical structure of pages, and *secondary* links may connect pages in an arbitrary way. The main reason for advocating a hierarchy of pages is that this kind of structure is easy to grasp for the visitor, as it is sufficiently simple and familiar ([RM02, p. 37]). Apart from that, a hierarchy also uniquely assigns a path to every page that can be used to construct URLs for them. Note that the hierarchical structure constitutes a backbone for the whole web site, and as such, its presence is vital. Additional links between pages that do not adhere to the hierarchy can be added at will, creating the secondary navigation structure *on top* of the primary one.

The visual notation is introduced in the following section 9.1 by taking the computer science faculty web site as an illustrating example. Section 9.2 then adds ideas concerning an automated mapping from the navigation structure to page functions. Section 9.3 concludes this chapter by completing the explanation of the navigation structure for the example web site.

9.1 Navigation Structure Diagrams

Figure 9.1 shows an example diagram that depicts the navigation structure used for the Computer Science Faculty web site.

Rounded rectangles represent web pages, black solid arcs define the hierarchy. The homepage is at level zero. Pages share one hierarchy level if they are reachable from the homepage along the shortest path of the same length using only black solid arcs. The hierarchy so defined is called the *primary navigation structure*. The pages are physically arranged according to this structure, and this also reflects in the URLs of the pages: the path through the hierarchy canonically corresponds to the path given in the URL.

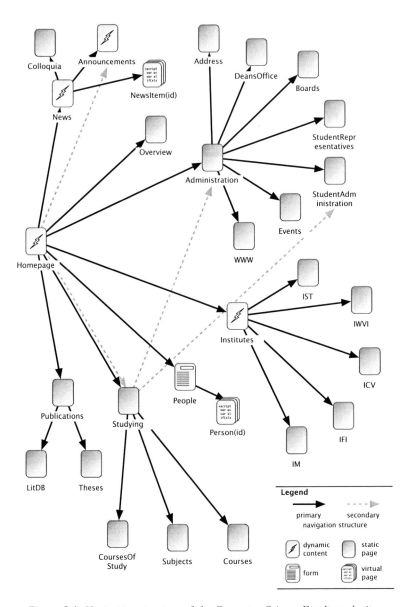

Figure 9.1: Navigation structure of the Computer Science Faculty web site

The page IST, for example, can be addressed via .../Homepage/Institutes/IST, with the ellipsis replaced by an appropriate prefix for the root of the homepage. On the actual web site, the primary navigation structure is visualised in a navigation menu on every page, in order to help the visitor find his or her current position inside the hierarchy. In addition to that, a *breadcrumbs*◇ trail shows the path of the current page in respect to the homepage, enabling the visitor to easily jump to any page on this path by simply activating the respective link. These links are not shown in the diagram.

Layered above the primary navigation structure is a second one, which is totally independent from the first. Any page can contain any number of hyperlinks to other pages, no matter where they are positioned in the hierarchy. The diagram captures these links with the dashed lines, that, as one can see, criss-cross the hierarchy without adhering to it. This does not exclude cases where a link in the second layer is coincidentally equivalent to one already defined in the primary navigation structure. One example is the link from the Homepage to the Studying page. Including links like this makes sense when the destination page should be accessible from multiple parts contained *inside* the origin page.

Web page icons come in different flavours, denoted by small 'adornments' to the rounded rectangles or by variants of the basic icon in the diagram.

- A lightning bolt marks a page that contains dynamically generated content. This includes content calculated according to parameters passed to the page (via CGI, for example) as well as content produced by any other kind of script that relies on the internal state of the system alone.

  News

- A form field on the page icon symbolises a page with some kind of web form. When the visitor submits the form, these pages call a script or another page that processes the data entered into the form. There may be more than one form on a page, but this fact will not be reflected in the page icon.

  People

- A small piece of script code on a stacked page icon signifies a *virtual* page that is computed by a script. In contrast to the 'lightning bolt' pages with dynamic content, the script-generated pages are *completely* calculated by a script that is provided with a set of parameters, where one (the first) parameter defines the name of the page. The virtual pages do not exist under a pre-defined identifier, like the pages with dynamic content do. They are rather created and evaluated on-the-fly, every time the script is called.

  Person(id)

These basic web page flavours can be mixed on one page. A virtual page or a dynamic page can contain a form (or more than one), and a virtual page is almost always dynamic. Since non-dynamic virtual pages do not make much sense – because this would mean that every instance looked the same and did not make use of the identifying parameter – the lightning bolt adornment will not be applied to virtual page icons, and virtual pages will count as *always* being dynamic.

The semantics of the links between pages can be further clarified by attaching symbols to them that define the *multiplicity* and the *permissions* necessary to use the respective link.

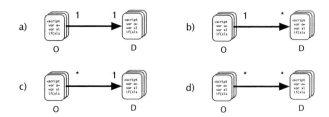

Figure 9.2: Multiplicity symbols for two virtual pages.

9.1.1 Multiplicity of primary navigation

Multiplicity symbols only apply to primary navigation links where at least one of the connected pages is a virtual page. The multiplicity then signifies how many links a page contains and where these links go to. There are three possible cases: both pages are virtual; only the origin page is virtual; or only the destination page is virtual. All three cases will be considered in turn. Clearly, pages can have any number of additional links, thus establishing the secondary navigation, but the cardinality given by the multiplicity symbols only refers to the *primary* navigation.

1. Origin and destination page are virtual

   Analogous to the multiplicity symbols in UML class diagrams, the multiplicity symbols used with links between two virtual pages denote the cardinality of the relationship between the instances. Here, *instance* refers to a virtual page instance, which will be simply called *page* in the following explanations.

   In general, the multiplicity symbol near the origin of the link defines whether there is *exactly one* origin page linking to a given destination page (symbolised by the digit '1'), or whether there is an *arbitrary number* of origin pages that link to this destination page (symbolised by an asterisk '*'). The symbol near the destination page tells whether the link destination is *specific* (symbol '1') or *arbitrary* (symbol '*'). Let O be the set of page instances of the origin page, and let D be the set of page instances of the destination page. The exact meanings of the multiplicities are as follows (cf. figure 9.2):

   a) 1—1

      Each of the origin page instances contains exactly one link. Each of these links goes to exactly one virtual page instance and there are no two links that go to the same instance. The mapping thus defined need not be bijective, however, because there may exist page instances that are no destination of any link:

      $$\forall o \in O : outdeg(o) = 1 \land \forall d \in D : indeg(d) \leq 1$$

      The functions *outdeg* and *indeg* denote the number of outgoing or incoming edges, respectively. In this context, we regard the virtual page instances as nodes and the link instances (primary navigation only) as edges.

This constellation can be used in practice when every instance of a virtual page is to be linked to one specific instance of another virtual page. The identifier of the origin page may then be used to address the destination page as well. This may happen after transforming the identifier through a bijective function, which in most cases will be the identity function, so that the same identifier is used to specify which virtual page instance shall be chosen.

An example is a virtual page with basic information about a person (Person(id), say) that links to a page with the publications of that particular person (PersonPublications(id)).

b) 1—*

Each of the origin page instances contains a list of links. On the destination side, the situation is the same as in case 1a: Each destination page is reached at most once. Since there are multiple links on each origin page instance, each origin page instance is allowed to be connected to a number of destination page instances.

$$\forall d \in D : indeg(d) \leq 1$$

An example is a virtual page that lists persons grouped by the first letter of their names with one page instance per letter. In these lists, there is one link for each person that leads to the respective home page.

c) *—1

Each of the origin page instances contains exactly one link. Each of these links goes to an arbitrary virtual page instance.

$$\forall o \in O : outdeg(o) = 1$$

The link destination is calculated arbitrarily.

An example is the page Person(id) with basic information about a person linking to a Department(id) page that is the homepage of this person's department. There may be any number of person pages that link to the same department page.

One could also think of a situation where the person page should link to *different* pages depending on the actual person. Some person pages could link to the corresponding department, but there may also be people who are not associated to any department at all (students or guest scientists, for example). For them, the link could go to a completely different page. The point is that the linked page itself may vary as well, i.e., the identifier of a link destination page (and not the page *instance*) may depend on some calculation. This implies a *dynamic* primary navigation structure. However, we will not allow arbitrarily calculated link destinations. It is o.k. to make a conditional expression that yields a link to one out of a set of possible destinations. In the navigation diagram, an arrow to each of the possible destinations will have to be drawn.

d) *—*

Figure 9.3: Multiplicity symbols for one virtual page on the origin side.

Each of the origin page instances contains a list of links, and the link destination is calculated arbitrarily. The link origins are grouped together on page instances, so each of the origin page instances links to a set of destination page instances.

There is no constraint on either $outdeg(o)$ or $indeg(d)$ for any o or d.

An example is a virtual page that lists postings in a news group. There is one page instance per news group, and each page instance contains a list of postings in this particular group. The postings are represented by the subject line, an each line links to another virtual page instance that shows detailed information about one posting. Taking into account the fact that one posting may appear in several news groups (cross posting), there may be more than one link to one particular posting, which makes it necessary to denote the link by '*—*' instead of '1—*'.

2. Only origin page is virtual

Again, the multiplicity on the origin side denotes a single link to the destination page ('1') or a number of links ('*'). The destination page can be a static, a dynamic, or a form page. All three page types can be treated the same at this point, and there is no need to use a multiplicity symbol on the destination side of the link, because there are no "instances" of the destination page. It can be regarded as a *singleton*. The exact meanings of the multiplicities are as follows (cf. figure 9.3):

a) 1—

Exactly one origin page instance links to the destination page.

It is hard to think of an example for this case, and it might not even appear in practice. It would mean that there is some kind of expression inside the description of the origin page that generates a link for one particular instance only.

b) *—

The destination page is linked to from a number of origin page instances.

An example is a virtual page that contains a link to a disclaimer page that applies to the whole site. Every page instance links to the (one and only) disclaimer page.

3. Only destination page is virtual

Figure 9.4: Multiplicity symbols for one virtual page on the destination side.

The multiplicity at the destination side specifies whether the origin page contains *one* link to a specific destination page instance (symbol '1') or a *list* of links (symbol '*'). The exact meanings of the multiplicities are as follows (cf. figure 9.4):

a) —1

> The origin page contains a link to a specific virtual page instance.
>
> An example might be a homepage of an institute containing a link to a fixed person page (Person(id) with some concrete id), e.g., the homepage of an affiliated scientist.

b) —*

> The origin page contains a list of links to a set of virtual page instances. Since the links will most probably be calculated, the origin page will be dynamic.
>
> An example might be a homepage of an institute with links to the institutes members' person pages (Person(id)).

Link parameters other than a virtual page identifier are not considered here, because they do not influence the multiplicity semantics.

9.1.2 Authorisation-dependent navigation

One needs to be able to protect content from being accessed by unauthorised web site visitors. Prerequisite for this is the application of authentication and authorisation techniques. For the web site model, authorisation information is relevant in order to capture which pages require what kind of permissions (cf. section 4.3 for a definition of the relevant terms). The navigation structure diagram may contain information on this authorisation-dependent navigation.

An arrow representing a link in the primary navigation structure may be equipped with a person-like icon (see figure 9.5 a)), a list of role identifiers and a scope designation. This symbolises that the destination page is *guarded* and that it can only be accessed if the current user has one of the roles listed.

If scope has the value subtree, which is the default, the authorisation constraint automatically expands to all pages that lie behind the destination page, i.e., one link with an authorisation constraint protects a whole subtree of the navigation hierarchy. This consequence can be inhibited by setting scope to thisPage, which makes the constraint apply to this page only.

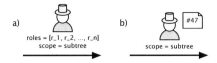

Figure 9.5: Guarded link.
a) Roles mentioned explicitly. b) Roles mentioned in an annotation.

Note that, although the authorisation constraint is attached to a link, this effectively protects the *page* this link goes to. This makes sense for primary navigation links, because the primary navigation structure is a tree, and there is always only one unique path to any page, so the page is unambiguously identified. As a consequence, the constraints do also apply when a page is accessed via any other link from *outside* the primary navigation structure. So, once a subtree in the primary navigation structure is protected by an authorisation-dependent link, any page somewhere inside this subtree is guarded by the same authorisation constraint as well.

Since the path to the root node of this tree is of length zero, the home page cannot be guarded by attaching some icon to an arrow, because there simply *is* no arrow to attach something to. This is not seen as a particularly dramatic defect, because protecting the whole web site by prohibitively disclosing the home page will be scarcely, if at all, found in practice. There should rather be at least one unguarded page that explains this fact to the visitor and that links to the first page of the protected area. This said, it should be pointed out that defining role restrictions and a scope designation for the web site's home page *is* possible, namely, by incorporating the corresponding function call into the page function that defines the home page's content. It is just that one cannot note this fact in the diagram.

If the web site visitor has not yet authenticated when accessing a page that requires a certain role, he or she will be asked to provide the necessary credentials. We suppose this is handled automatically by the implementation platform by instructing the web server to send back a corresponding HTTP message (code 401: Unauthorised) to the client. If the login attempt fails, the originally requested page will not be delivered and an error code (code 403: Forbidden) will be sent back to the browser instead.

In the general case, a link to a guarded page will appear in the origin page like any other link. If the link shall be hidden or otherwise treated differently when the visitor is actually not entitled to see the corresponding destination page, this must be included in the page function definition by querying the current visitor data.

Sometimes, a more fine-grained control of authorisation is needed. We assume that the implementation platform provides means to set up and control permissions on a more detailed level. For this text, a simple authorisation model is proposed that may be superseded by the possibilities of the implementation platform. Our model demands for a set of *permissions* that can be granted to *roles* on an *object* level. An object in this case is any page generating function.

Identifier	Permission
ViewPage	View the given page (i.e., evaluate the page function)
ViewPageAttributes	View any page attribute

Table 9.1: Permissions for web pages

#47	$Role_1$	$Role_2$	$Role_3$
ViewPage	Y	Y	N
ViewPageAttributes	N	Y	Y

Table 9.2: Example permission annotation for a web page

Table 9.1 lists the minimal set of permissions that can be granted to roles. The ViewPage permission is the *default* permission. An authorisation-dependent link, via the list of role identifiers, always refers to this permission if nothing else is said. Its purpose is to disallow an unauthorised visitor to *see* a particular page. This is achieved by inhibiting the evaluation of the corresponding page function.

Apart from that, one could also want to constrain the access to the page's attributes, like the title. This is the purpose of the ViewPageAttributes permission. Requiring appropriate authorisation for seeing the title of a page means that the page could not even appear in a list of pages (e.g., inside a navigation menu or a *site map*$^\diamond$) without the visitor being properly authenticated. This way, the mere existence of a page can be veiled unless the visitor is allowed to be aware of it.

Other permissions than these two may be realised by the implementation platform and then they, too, may be used in the model. For our purpose, it is sufficient that there exists a function that returns either True or False when given a specific visitor, a specific permission and a specific page, thus telling whether or not, respectively, the visitor is in possession of that permission for the given page.

To specify the relation of permissions and roles for a particular page in the model, an annotation to the diagram is to be given. The annotation should be made in form of a table that details which permission shall be granted to which role. The table can be placed into the diagram (by attaching a note sheet to the link with a dashed line, as is usual in UML diagrams), but this will in most cases make the diagram too cluttered. Instead, the existence of an annotation is signalled by a small adornment to the icon, a small sheet of paper with a number inside (see figure 9.5 b)), and the annotation itself is stated somewhere else, e.g., in the accompanying text. If an annotation is present, the list of roles at the link symbol, specifying which roles have got the ViewPage permission, is superfluous and must be omitted.

The actual table is an $p \times r$ matrix, where p is the number of permissions, and r is the number of roles. Table 9.2 shows a schematic example. In the upper left-hand corner, the table contains a numerical identifier that is referenced in the corresponding link symbol in the diagram. Each inner table cell contains either Y or N. The letter Y means that, for the given page, the permission in the current row is *granted* to visitors having the role mentioned in the current column's header. Contrariwise, N signifies that the permission is *not* granted.

In order to make the tables more readable even when a greater number of permissions is involved, one can define rules that allow to leave out unnecessary table rows, for example by claiming that if a particular permission is not mentioned in the table (i.e., when the corresponding row is missing), the permission/role assignment is to be taken from the parent page, recursively. This would mean that the tables only have to specify those constraints that differ from the previous hierarchy level. In order for this chain to be well-defined, the top-most page (i.e., the homepage) would have to have an annotation that defines defaults for all of the permissions. These defaults might be to allow everything, i.e., every permission is granted to every role. Rules like that may be put in place *on top* of what is specified in this text, as long as they comply to the model proposed here and given that every addition can be re-mapped to a specification that adheres to the simple rules used throughout this text.

9.2 From Navigation Structure to Page Functions

We have seen how to use functions to describe the abstract structure of web pages. Link nodes and form nodes can be included in the APD structures to implement the navigation structure of the web site. The navigation structure, however, was *modelled* using a navigation structure diagram, showing the interconnection between pages. This diagram also helped in identifying the primary and secondary navigation structure. The definition of the single pages as functions is carried out *only after* the navigation structure is available. This section presents ideas showing how to automatically *derive* the page functions from the navigation structure.

A navigation structure diagram (see figure 9.1 for an example) specifies a tree of pages (the primary navigation structure) as well as a second layer of links between pages (the secondary navigation structure). The direction of the links is symbolised by the arrowheads. So, for any given page, it is possible to determine the set of outgoing links and the corresponding set of target pages.

Furthermore, the diagram states the identifiers of the pages, and it shows which pages contain forms and which pages are virtual.

Using this information, it is possible to present an algorithm that produces one function definition for each page in the diagram. These APD-generating functions are mere page 'skeletons' and will only contain Link and Form elements. Beyond that, the pages will be empty, and the functions have to be filled with the intended APD-generating expressions.

The links generated by the algorithm are equipped with a unique identifier, an empty list of attributes, an empty list of child nodes, and the identifier of the target page function. No distinction is made between links belonging to the primary or secondary navigation structure.

Form elements are generated likewise. The form action page, however, is left empty, because the diagram does not specify where the form data is to be sent to. An arc in the diagram leaving a page with a form is assumed to be a normal link, because there is no telling of whether it has got anything to do with the form. Since there might be more than one form on the page, it is not clear where the link actually originates from.

This way, page functions and functions for virtual pages can be constructed that are guaranteed to reflect the modelled navigation structure. The functions, once available, can be extended manually to return the corresponding APD structure that is wanted for the particular page. It is also possible to write a function that automatically checks whether the pages still contain the link structure originally devised[1]. This can be done by traversing the APD structures and checking whether links and forms are supplied with the correct target functions.

Note that this checking cannot, in the general case, be applied to the multiplicities defined for virtual pages. If the system does not prevent manual alterations of the expressions that calculate link destinations, it is not possible to test whether the link destination is specific, i.e., whether or not the expression evaluates to the same value for any given argument. Turning the argument around, we can state that it is possible to guarantee that the initially generated page skeletons contain only valid links, but that it is the obligation of the concrete implementation to either prevent further edits, or leave it up to the designer to refine link definitions under his or her own responsibility.

9.3 Navigation Structure for the Example Web Site

The navigation structure of the faculty web site is basically hierarchical. Figure 9.1 showed this hierarchy's first three levels. The top-most document in the hierarchy is the homepage, which is positioned near the left edge of the diagram, and the hierarchy unfolds from left to right.

---

[1] The evaluation of this check must depend on static values (i.e., constants) only

Presentation Functions

The obligation of the presentation functions is to specify the *design* of the final pages with respect to their representation in the chosen output language. The pages, as described by the page functions, are given as abstract terms that adhere to the abstract page description (APD) data type. In order to generate a version that can be sent to a requesting client, this abstract representation has got to be transformed into a concrete form. Clearly, the actual output language depends on what was laid down in the requirements for the web application. Using presentation *functions*, the full range of flexibility is open to create the output that is needed, be it XHTML, or any other XML dialect, or even any other language that uses a different syntax.

As XHTML is the prominent output language used for current web applications, we will focus on this language as our example vehicle. In principle, of course, any other language could have been used as well.

The following section 10.1 introduces the presentation functions in general terms. Section 10.2 then highlights the possibilities and challenges of producing context-aware web sites. Section 10.3 shows example presentation functions for the computer science faculty web site.

10.1 Getting it out

A presentation function maps an APD term to a term in the desired output language. The output language can be any language whatsoever. There is also no need to constrain oneself to using only *one* output language for the whole web site. In principle, due to the employment of a functional programming language, the output can be varied, depending on any information accessible at the time of the evaluation of the respective presentation function. The implied flexibility is exploited to create context-aware web sites, whose description is deferred until the following section. The current section considers only web sites using *one* output language consistently for all pages.

As was already pointed out, the choice of output languages is arbitrary. The first and obvious selection might therefore be using the APD itself as the output language. This is not very realistic, however, since this would require an user agent that could render pages described as APD terms as well as an agreement on a concrete element structure of the pages and their respective graphical representation. This, however, would confine the usefulness to those user agents, which effectively do not exist. The standard languages for the dissemination of web pages are the variants of XHTML or other XML languages for mobile devices, and we do not strive at inventing a replacement for those.

Agreeing on using XML as the output language, the transformation that has to be performed by the presentation function can be expressed by a mapping of APD elements to XML elements, or by any other mapping of whole APD terms to XML elements.

In order to generate the final result, it is also possible to perform additional transformation steps *after* the presentation functions have been evaluated. Depending on the available technology in the implementation platform or on particular requirements regarding the presentation, the generated output may be subjected to further conversions. When using XML as the output language, for example, one can use XSLT ([Cla99]) to define further transformations, be it on the client side or on the server side. This adds yet another level of abstraction, and it may be worthwhile to take advantage of it, in particular when it comes to the integration of the produced pages with pages that are generated by other systems that offer no other means to do so. In general, however, it is advisable to stay inside the system as described in this text and to perform all of the necessary transformations with the presentation functions. This fosters coherency, because it is not necessary to use a 'foreign' language (like XSLT), and at the same time does not prevent the introduction of further abstraction levels.

As a rule of thumb, the presentation functions should be as simple as possible. If the mapping gets too complex, it should be modularised by composing functions that each perform a designated part of the work.

10.2 Contextuality

Because of the high flexibility that is offered by the fact that presentation functions can do *any* transformation of the APD terms before producing the actual output, the presentation functions are good candidates for the inclusion of context-aware features. The presentation functions should always concentrate on the presentation only (hence their name), so they should not be used to drastically change the page layout or the page content, which might be necessary in the course of evaluation of the context and the implementation of adaptation. However, some adaptations are strictly presentational, and they should be included in the presentation functions.

As an example, consider the adaptation towards specific output languages or towards output devices with limited or differing capabilities. The presentation function can check the current context that is given to them via their arguments, and can produce corresponding output according to the result of these checks.

10.3 Presentation Functions for the Example Web Site

In the example page functions shown in section 8.7, the produced APD terms were already very close to XHTML in that the identifiers for APD elements were mostly equivalent to existing XHTML element names. It was argued in section 8.3 that there should be a consistent APD element structure throughout the pages, which significantly eases the transformation into an output language like XHTML. This holds particularly when the element structure is already this close to the output language. In our example, we can therefore get along with a very simple and straightforward transformation of the APD terms: except for Link and Form elements, we simply serialise the term as an XML document. The function

```
linksToHTMLElements :: APD → (Identifier → String) → APD
linksToHTMLElements n@(Text s) _ = n
linksToHTMLElements (Element n a es) id2url =
   Element n a (map (λe → linksToHTMLElements e id2url) es)
linksToHTMLElements (Link n a es pid pa) id2url =
   Element "a" ([ ("href", (id2url pid)++(paramsToURI pa)) ] ++ a) es
linksToHTMLElements (Form n a es pid pa) id2url =
   Element "form"
     (
       [ ("name", n)
       , ("method", "post")
       , ("action", (id2url pid)++(paramsToURI pa))
       ]
       ++ a
     )
     (map (λe → linksToHTMLElements e id2url) es)
linksToHTMLElements f@(Field n a es s) id2url = fieldsToHTMLElements f
linksToHTMLElements x _ = x −−−Empty
```

performs the necessary transformations. It relies on a function id2url that has to be passed as a parameter which generates a valid URL for a given page function identifier. The function fieldsToHTMLElements generates XHTML elements that correspond to the diverse types of form input fields, like option lists or text inputs.

The APD term generated by linksToHTMLElements contains Element terms only, so the creation of XML is as simple as the recursive traversal of the term and the construction of a string that represents the final XML document. Section 14.2 in the appendix gives a full account on the necessary steps to produce deliverable XML.

The Travel Agency System Example

As a proof of concept, the approach described in this thesis shall be applied to a second example, in addition to the computer science faculty web site: a simple travel agency system, henceforward abbreviated with TAS. This system is of a different kind, compared to the faculty web site, because the TAS puts more emphasis on the business logic and it is more application-like than the first example. Therefore, the TAS poses a different kind of challenge, and successfully meeting these requirements demonstrates the versatility and completeness of our approach. In addition, this second example will be presented 'in one go', allowing for a fluent following of the necessary steps, without interspersed explanations of aspects belonging to the approach itself.

The TAS described in the following is not related to any existing system of comparable orientation, it is, in the end, a 'toy' example. It draws most of its central requirements from [TAS05], a concise description of a fictive travel agency system, offering a level of complexity that was just about right to suggest that the system could be used as an example in this text. The requirements stated there are completed at some points and clarified at others, in order to be able give a *formal* specification of the TAS.

The TAS is a web application that helps web site visitors in booking trips. It concentrates on transportation services using planes, trains, cars, boats, or combinations thereof. Add-ons like accommodation or the arrangement of sightseeing tours are not part of the system. As the TAS is a commercial system, we will use the term *customer* in addition to *visitor* when speaking about the person who uses the web site.

The TAS web site is the interface to the customer. The web site *represents* the travel agency. The TAS encompasses back-end operations like managing a customer database, forwarding a customer's request to broker agents, handling of billing information and co-operation with financial institutions.

The following section 11.1 will provide detailed information on the participating actors, followed by the content model in section 11.2. After that, section 11.3 will report on the non-functional requirements as well as on the central scenario that provides the essential functional requirements and explains how the system should work. The scenario description is distilled into a set of functions that capture the system's services in a more formal way (section 11.4). This is followed by the navigation model (navigation structure and page functions, described in sections 11.5 and 11.6, respectively), the

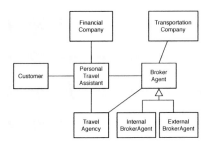

Figure 11.1: Actors and their relationships for the TAS example
(syntax: UML class diagram)

accompanying queries (section 11.8), and finally some notes concerning the presentation model in section 11.9.

11.1 Actors

The participants in the TAS are depicted in the class diagram in figure 11.1. It shows the actors as classes and the interaction between them as associations.

A short description of the actors follows.

Customer A *customer* (C) is the web site visitor who uses the web site to provide a trip description (including constraints), to receive trip suggestions and to pay for and book trips. A customer provides a trip description comprising the relevant calendar dates, the origin and the destination city, and a set of preferences and constraints, like the dislike of specific transportation means or a temporal bound on the overall trip duration.

PersonalTravelAssistant A *personal travel assistant* (PTA) is the 'interface' to the customer and, from the customer's perspective, it represents the entire web application and it also represents the travel agency.

TravelAgency A *travel agency* (TA) is a company that 'runs' the TAS. It provides the services to the customer through the web application, i.e., through the personal travel assistant. It co-operates with broker agents.

BrokerAgent A *broker agent* (BA) is a mediator between travel agencies and transportation companies. The broker agent is asked by a personal travel assistant to provide an offer for a concrete combination of transportation services in order to fulfil a given trip specification. This act of combining is regarded to be the main business logic of the whole TAS. A travel agency can either use internal broker agents or it

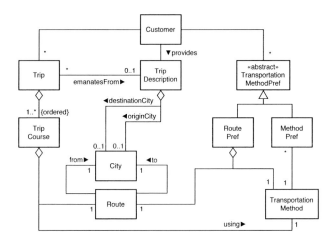

Figure 11.2: Classes and relationships for the TAS example
(syntax: UML class diagram)

can delegate the work to external broker agents that are situated in other travel
agencies.

TransportationCompany A *transportation company* (TC) provides transportation services, that is, the transportation of one customer from a city A to a city B using a
specific means of transportation (plane, train, car, boat). The actual transportation
service may be performed by a company (e.g., car rental, airline) on behalf of the
transportation company. These companies are out of the scope of the TAS, and we
pretend that the transportation service is offered by the transportation company.

FinancialCompany A *financial company* (FC) is in charge of providing the necessary
financial services. The personal travel agent forwards the payment information
given by the customer to a financial company, which in turn settles the payment
with the travel agency.

From the description of the actors, we can extract a first set of architectural building
blocks. Figure 11.1 visualises these blocks by showing four grey-shaded areas. The
biggest area represents the 'travel agency' as seen from the customer's perspective. It
comprises the TravelAgency, PersonalTravelAssistant, and the three BrokerAgent classes. The
Customer, FinancialCompany and the TransportationCompany are distinct entities of their
own.

11.2 Content Model

The content model captures the entities of the application domain and their relationships. For the TAS example, we regard just a section of the application domain: The diagram in figure 11.2 contains classes that deal with the description of a trip and the storage of a customer's preferences in terms of transportation methods and routes. A detailed description of the classes follows. The diagram does not mention any attributes, they were omitted for better readability. The following text introduces them along with the classes. Class identifiers start with a capital letter, while attribute identifiers, as well as association names, start with a lower case one.

A customer (Customer) is an authenticated web site visitor. For simplicity, the only attributes are a unique user name (name) and a password (password). Customers are entitled to have their preferences stored (abstract class TransportationMethodPref). This is expressed by the existence of one or many associated instances of MethodPref and RoutePref.

The presence of a method preference (MethodPref) states that a specific transportation method (TransportationMethod) is acceptable for the customer. This means that in order to express that the customer does *not* like a certain transportation method, all *but* the affected transportation method must be listed. In addition, we define that if *no* method preference is given for a customer, then *any* transportation method is acceptable for that customer.

A route preference (RoutePref) allows the customer to define that a given route should only be travelled using specific transportation methods. In other words, the customer can state that a method preference applies to a specific route only. A route (Route) is the interconnection of two cities, the origin and the destination. A city (City) is identified by its name (id).

A customer provides trip descriptions (TripDescription). They state the date and city of departure (dateOfDeparture, originCity), the destination city (destinationCity), and a return date (dateOfReturn). The return date may be omitted for a one-way trip. A trip description furthermore comprises trip constraints and trip sorting preferences. Trip constraints may include one or both of the following: (1) an upper limit on the total price of the trip (maxTotalPrice); (2) an upper limit on the total duration of the trip (maxTotalDuration). Trip sorting preferences state in which order matching trips shall be presented to the customer, i.e., whether they shall be sorted by their total price, or by their total duration (sortBy).

After a trip description is submitted by the customer, the system produces one or more concrete trips (Trip). A trip has a total price (totalPrice) and a total duration (totalDuration). It comprises a succession of courses (TripCourse), i.e., concrete routes travelled using concrete transportation methods.

11.3 Non-functional and Functional Requirements

The TAS should meet the following *non-functional requirements*: usability, efficiency, reliability, scalability, and security. Without any further specification, these requirements are not acceptable to be included in the requirements catalogue. Rather, a precise definition of the kinds of *measurements* and of the required results must be provided. For efficiency, for example, one could specify that the system should be able to serve a given number of parallel sessions without any user experiencing recognisable latency. Concrete figures would be stated as parts of the requirements, together with the test specification that prescribed which simulations had to be performed and how the measurement results had to be obtained.

However, specifying these kinds of requirements at this level of detail is out of the scope for our TAS example. In general, one can say that usability and efficiency concerns can hardly be covered by the models and specifications we are providing at this stage, because both rely on implementation specific qualities. As far as reliability is concerned, one can only say that the functional specifications are inherently sound, and that the final system can be made as reliable as the specifications, provided that the actual implementation does not introduce any new sources of unreliability. Scalability, too, is only constrained by the implementation platform, as the specification does not include anything that *prevents* the system from being scalable. Security, finally, must be enforced by the implementation as well. This includes the encryption of data as soon as that data leaves the system. Since our approach abstracts from the underlying implementation as far as possible, introducing features like encrypted data transfer between the web browser and the web server does not affect the rest of the system.

The *functional requirements* of the TAS shall be provided by presenting one typical usage scenario, including the most typical exceptions. It is to be noted, however, that the following description does not suffice to specify the system in its entirety; rather, it is *part* of the specification. Additional scenarios as well as use case descriptions would have to be provided if this were a *real* requirements documentation. Instead, together with this scenario description, the models and specifications presented in the remainder of this chapter also constitute the requirements, rather than being *derived* from them. The text margin contains the names of identified business logic functions that will be referred to in section 11.4.

Our scenario involves a customer, she is called Alice, who wishes to book a trip by using the web site. The viewpoint used for the description shifts between the customer's and the systems', because the inner workings of the system are precluded from the customer, but their unveiling is important and essential for the scenario description to be useful as a source for defining the required functionality.

Alice is in her office and she is using her desktop computer to browse the web. She accesses the TAS home page and clicks on the link to the page where she can enter a trip description. Alice is planning to travel from Tokyo to New York on the 23rd of December, and she wants to make sure that an acceptable flight is available. She enters the date of departure and picks the origin and the destination city from the lists of cities. Since this will be a one-way trip, she leaves the return date field empty. She does not care about the option to provide a limit for the overall trip duration, but she *does* enter a value into the field for the maximum allowed price for the trip. The form also offers her to specify the sorting order for the trip list that will get displayed later on. She does not really care, so she keeps the default value. If Alice were authenticated, her current user preferences regarding her acceptable transportation methods would be listed as well. She would also see a link to a page called 'edit your personal preferences' that she could use to have her preferred ways of transportation stored. At this time, however, she does not want to do that, and she premisses that, for her trip from Tokyo to New York, any other transportation method apart from planes will not be considered anyway. She submits the form.

check-
Wellformedness
The personal travel assistant receives the form data and checks it for well-formedness. This includes syntax-checking the values given for the date fields, checking for inequality of origin and destination city, as well as checking whether the date of return is later than the date of departure, which does not apply for Alice's request since she did not supply a return date in the

prepareTrips
findTripOffers
first place. All checks are passed, and the personal travel agent selects one broker agent and asks it for an offer that fulfils Alice's trip description. The broker agent contacts two transportation companies that are able to serve the

select-
Transportation-
Company
request, and receives three different flight offers. The broker agent's decision about which transportation companies to address is based upon 'internal knowledge' of the agent, and the definition of the corresponding rules is not part of the system specification. The transportation companies temporarily

bookTemporarily
calculateTotal-
Price
book the respective flights. The broker agent passes the three offers back to the personal travel assistant, along with the corresponding price information. For this particular trip, it was not necessary to combine separate offers in order to cover the requested route. In the general case, however, it is the

splitTrip
broker agent's obligation to deliver coherent offers for a trip that involves multiple stations and multiple transportation methods. The personal travel assistant thus always receives complete offers.

checkTrip-
Constraints
cancelTrip
The personal travel assistant rejects one of the three offers because its price is higher than the limit given by the customer. The broker agent is informed about this fact, and it forwards this cancellation to the transportation company

revokeBooking
sortTrips
that had offered and temporarily booked the flight, so it can revoke the booking. The personal travel assistant sorts the remaining two offers according to their price in ascending order, because Alice did not specify otherwise. The two flights are presented to Alice on a web page that lists the flight itineraries, comprising the dates, the names of the airlines, and the prices.

Alice chooses the cheaper of the two offers and clicks on the corresponding link that leads her to a page providing detailed information about this flight. In addition to the data showed on the page before, this page informs about fees and taxes, and it also includes a current weather report for the destination city, New York. The weather report captures Alice's attention for a while, but she realises that the probability of the temperatures staying at around 30°C until December is not very high. She sighs. — Nevertheless, she decides to take this flight, and she clicks on the button that takes her to the form to enter the billing details. She fills in the required personal data and submits the form.

The personal travel assistant receives the data and asks the financial company to confirm the payment. As a matter of fact, the financial company refuses the payment because the given credit card number is not valid. A corresponding error message is sent back to Alice, asking her to validate the data she entered into the form.

confirmPayment

check-
CreditCardNumber

Alice realises that she had overlooked to pick the right credit card company. She corrects her selection and resubmits the form. This time, the payment is confirmed and Alice receives an order confirmation on the next page. She uses her web browser's *print* command to print a hardcopy of that confirmation.

cancelTrip,
revokeBooking
(s.a.)

The personal travel assistant informs the broker agent about Alice's final choice, which results in the broker agent cancelling the booking for the rejected offer.

11.4 Dynamics

The behavioural aspect of the TAS can be modelled elegantly by looking at the different basic functions that have to carried out by the actors. Thus, the 'business logic' is broken down into well-specified functions that can be glued together in the page function definitions or by distinguished 'business logic functions', whose responsibility it is to combine basic functions and to define a control flow from one page function to the next. The usage scenario is a good source for finding functions of this kind; the previous section has already given their identifiers in the margin, near the position where the respective functionality is mentioned for the first time.

In the following, we will consider some of the functions in more detail. Each will be introduced by a tabular profile. It states the name and type of the function as well as the function provider (the abbreviations are defined in section 11.1). The rows marked 'In' and 'Out' describe the input and output parameters, respectively. The entry marked 'Descr' provides a short description of the function's semantics. Identifiers that are referred to appear in the content model (cf. section 11.2), some additional ones are below. The functions will be specified formally by giving respective definitions in Haskell, which are given by the 'Def' entry. Thus, they can be used directly in the page functions. This emphasises their versatility, being specification and implementation at the same time.

The parameter types used in the function signatures have to be mapped to Haskell data types. It should be pointed out that this will imply slight deviations from the initial, object oriented model. This is due to the fact that the data types in Haskell will be *regular*. The deviations are, however, of no *conceptual* relevance, and they are of a straightforward manner. For example, associations between classes will be modelled by sub-terms, which corresponds to introducing new attributes into one (or both) of the classes, depending on the multiplicity of the associations. Furthermore, some parameter types reflect the data structure that is used to pass values from a form to a corresponding action function. Since the format used on the forms may differ from that found in the conceptual model, conversions will be applied here as well. The following examples will hopefully further clarify these issues.

All functions needing access to the instance graph and the session data, including authentication information, demand an argument of the type SessionContext (see section 8.4). If the state is changed by a function, then it returns the new state information. If a function evokes side-effects apart from changing the internal state, e.g., by calling external services, it must return a value of type Stateful a, where a is the actual return type, which allows to perform any operations inside the **IO** monad via liftIO.

The function checkWellformedness has the following profile:

Name:	checkWellformedness :: TripDescriptionRecord → **Bool**
By:	PTA (personal travel assistant)
In:	trip description (TripDescriptionRecord)
Out:	true, if trip description is well-formed, i.e., plausible; false, otherwise. checkWellformedness does not return the *reason* for a failure.
Descr:	Checks a trip description for plausibility. In order to qualify as such, all of the following conditions must be met:

- The cities denoted by originCity and destinationCity are not equal.

- dateOfReturn is later than dateOfDeparture

Def:	checkWellformedness :: TripDescriptionRecord → **Bool**
	 checkWellformedness td =
	 (originCity td ≠ destinationCity td)
	 && (
	     if (**isJust** (dateOfReturn td)) *-- is the return date provided at all?*
	     then (**fromJust** (dateOfReturn td) > (dateOfDeparture td))
	     else True
	)

The input parameter type is given by the following two declarations:

```
data TripSortingPreference = SortByPrice | SortByDuration
data TripDescriptionRecord = TripDescriptionRecord
  { originCity :: City
  , destinationCity :: City
  , dateOfDeparture :: CalendarTime
  , dateOfReturn :: Maybe CalendarTime
  , maxTotalPrice :: Maybe Num
  , maxTotalDuration :: Maybe TimeDiff
  , sortingPreference :: TripSortingPreference
  } deriving Show
```

This is a record-like data type with labelled constructor arguments. The TripDescription-Record data constructor accepts seven arguments, which directly correspond to the form fields on the page that lets the customer supply the trip description. In the content model, the fact that a trip description includes the notion of the destination city is captured by the destinationCity association between TripDescription and City. The *data type* TripDescriptionRecord, however, has a *field* instead. Thus, a term for a concrete trip description will have a sub-expression of type City at this position. The latter type is given by

```
data City = City {cityName :: String} deriving (Show, Eq)
```

The function prepareTrips is given as follows:

Name:	prepareTrips :: TripDescriptionRecord → SessionContext → [TripRecord]
By:	PTA (personal travel assistant)
In:	trip description (TripDescriptionRecord), session information
Out:	ordered list of trips that match the trip description ([TripRecord])
Descr:	Processes a well-formed trip description and presents a list of matching trips. The list is generated by this (very inefficient) algorithm:

1. find all sequences of routes, such that they start at the origin city and end at the destination city
2. for each route, retrieve the set of possible transportation methods; this is achieved by looking for corresponding instances of TripCourse
3. generate one TripRecord object for each possible route and transportation method
4. if the request belongs to a recognised customer, eliminate trips that contain trip courses which are not acceptable according to this customer's transportation method preferences
5. call function findTripOffers, i.e., ask the broker agent to check for actual trips offered by transportation companies; this may add further trips in the case that one transportation company offers more than one suggestion to travel one trip course (e.g., one flight in the morning, another in the afternoon)
6. call function sortTrips, i.e., build the final list of trips by sorting them according the sorting preferences given in the TripDescriptionRecord

Def: ... −− *omitted*

This is the 'big' function that combines every necessary step to transform a trip description given by a customer into a list of proper trip offers. The trips in this list are temporarily booked by the participating transportation companies. When the customer selects one of these trips, the other preliminary bookings must be revoked by the broker agent.

The type TripRecord used in the signature to form the list of resulting trips conveys enough information to represent one particular trip (the trip course, the routes and transportation methods). It's definition is not given here. Confer the content model (section 11.2) for a description of the corresponding Trip class.

The function findTripOffers is given by:

Name:	findTripOffers :: [TripRecord] → [TripRecord]
By:	BA (broker agent)
In:	list of trips ([TripRecord])
Out:	list of offered, temporarily booked trips ([TripRecord])
Descr:	Generates a list of confirmed trip offers for a given list of trips. For each trip in the initial list, transportation companies are asked to offer and temporarily book the respective transportation method. If a transportation company can make more than one offer for a given trip course, the whole trip is duplicated for each offer. Thus, the resulting list of trips may be longer than the original one.
Def:	... -- *omitted*

The function calculateTotalPrice is defined by:

Name:	calculateTotalPrice :: TripRecord → Stateful **Double**
By:	BA (broker agent)
In:	trip (TripRecord)
Out:	the total price for this trip (a value of type **Double**)
Descr:	Calculates the sum of prices for the given trip. The trip may contain any number of trip courses, i.e., routes and associated transportation methods. The broker agent requests the price information from transportation companies it co-operates with.
Def:	... -- *omitted*

The function sortTrips is defined by:

Name:	sortTrips :: [TripRecord] → TripDescriptionRecord → [TripRecord]
By:	PTA (personal travel assistant)
In:	list of trips ([TripRecord]), trip description (TripDescriptionRecord)
Out:	list of trips ([TripRecord]), ordered by the field specified in the trip description
Descr:	Sorts items in the list of trips according to the sorting order preference given in the trip description. The trips can be sorted by their total price or by their total duration.
Def:	sortTrips :: [TripRecord] → TripDescriptionRecord → [TripRecord]
	sortTrips ts td =
	case (sortingPreference td) **of**
	SortByPrice → quicksortMap totalPrice ts
	SortByDuration → quicksortMap totalDuration ts

The function quicksortMap used in the specification sorts a given list, but applies the function given as its first argument to every element in the list and compares the function results instead of the original values.

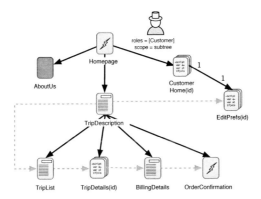

Figure 11.3: Navigation structure for the TAS example (syntax: cf. section 9.1)

11.5 Navigation Structure

In order to get a first impression on the structure of the web site, the navigation structure is presented *before* defining the page functions in the following section.

From the home page (Homepage), the web site visitor can access a static page with information about the travel agency (AboutUs).

The page called TripDescription is the entry point into the web site area where a customer can order trips. The customer can enter a trip description and trip constraints. If the customer is authenticated prior to accessing this page, his or her stored trip preferences will be displayed as well, and a link to EditPref(id) will lead to the page where these preferences can be edited. The four pages on the tree level below TripDescription, i.e., TripList, TripDetails(id), BillingDetails, and OrderConfirmation, are designed to be accessed in just this order (thus, they form a *guided tour* [GPS93]). Following this trail, the customer can pick a trip from a list of possibilities that match the trip description, review the details of the selected trip, provide the billing information, and finally submit the order, which is confirmed by giving a summary on the last page. The customer can quit at any time, or resume to the first page to refine or change the trip description or the preferences.

The page CustomerHome(id) is a personalised 'home' page for a customer with some user name id, where he or she can check the current status of any pending order and see the discounts he or she is eligible to. Any other personalised content could be added as needed, including customisable parts. The page also contains a link to EditPref(id). This page is used to review and modify the customer's preferences.

11.6 Page Functions

This section presents selected page functions. We have chosen not to provide all functions, but to constrain ourselves to the most interesting ones. It is particularly noteworthy that the page functions take full advantage of the possibility to access and modify the internal *state*, which consists of the data graph and the session data. This is the reason for them to be of type StatefulPageFunc, which implies that the monadic **do**-notation can be used to thread the state through the individual function calls.

As was done for the computer science faculty web site, the page functions defined for the TAS make use of a page template that defines the general layout of all pages. The page template is defined by the function tasMainTemplate, which offers the same slots as fb4MainTemplate did, i.e., heading, navigation, body, and footer. The code for tasMainTemplate is not given here, as it does not offer anything new. The reader is kindly referred to section 8.5 for an explanation of the templating mechanism.

The TripDescription page contains a form for the actual trip description. The page is defined by the following function tasTripDescription:

```
tasTripDescription :: StatefulPageFunc
tasTripDescription params = do
   (graph, session) ← get
   navigation ← tasNavigation params
   tdForm ← tasTripDescriptionForm []                                    (1)
   prefList ← tasPreferencesList params
   prefLink ← return $ if (hasAttr session "customerId")
      then [Link "toEditPrefs" [] [] "tasEditPrefs"  [("id", getValue session "customerId" )] ]
      else []
   return $ tasMainTemplate
      ( Element "slots" []
         [ Element "heading" [] [Text "Trip␣Description"]
         , Element "navigation" [] [ navigation ]
         , Element "body" []
            ([ tdForm                                                    (2)
            , prefList
            ]
            ++ prefLink)
         , Element "footer" [] [ Text "Footer" ]
         ])
```

The form is defined by a separate function, tasTripDescriptionForm, which is explained below. The APD returned by that function is bound to the variable tdForm in the line marked by (1), which is then used in the actual page construction at position (2). Analogously, the list of the current customer's preferences is included by calling the function tasPreferencesList, also explained later on. The third ingredient for the TripDescription page is a link to the EditPrefs(id) page, where the customer can edit his or her preferences. This link is only visible if the current session contains a reference to an authenticated customer.

The actual entry form is provided by the page fragment tasTripDescriptionForm. Before constructing the form structure, it retrieves the list of all possible origin cities and destination cities by performing corresponding queries.

```
tasTripDescriptionForm :: StatefulPageFunc
tasTripDescriptionForm _ = do
   (graph, session) ← get
   return $
      let
         originCities = concatMap (++ "\n") $ getOriginCities graph
         destCities = concatMap (++ "\n") $ getDestCities graph
      in
         Form "TripDescriptionForm" []
            [ Text "From:"
            , Field "originCity" [("type", "optionlist"), ("values", originCities)] [] ""
            , Text "To:"
            , Field "destCity" [("type", "optionlist"), ("values", destCities)] [] ""
            , Text "Departure:"
            , Field "dateOfDeparture" [] [] ""
            , Text "Return:"
            , Field "dateOfReturn" [] [] ""
            , Text "Maximum␣Price:"
            , Field "maxTotalPrice" [] [] ""
            , Text "Maximum␣Duration:"
            , Field "maxTotalDuration" [] [] ""
            , Text "Sorting␣Order:"
            , Field "sortingPreference"
                [("type", "optionlist"), ("values", "SortByPrice\nSortByDuration")] [] ""
            , Field "submit" [("type","submit")] [] ""
            ]
            "tasTripList" []
```

The list of preferences of a customer consists of the respective transportation methods he or she accepts. The following functions retrieves them accordingly:

```
tasPreferencesList :: StatefulPageFunc
tasPreferencesList params = do
   (graph, session) ← get
   return $
      let
         methodPrefs = getMethodPrefs graph (valueForParam "customerId" params)
      in
         foreach
            methodPrefs
            (Element "list" [] [])
            (λ methodName →
                Element "item" [] [ Text methodName ]
            )
```

The preceding definition makes use of the foreach construct that allows to conveniently iterate over the list of method preferences. It produces one item element for each member of that list. The produced list will be empty if no customer was given or if there were no preferences set for the customer.

In order to validate the parameters that are supplied via the form on the TripDescription page, the following function validateTripDescription converts a given set of parameters, i.e., simple, string-based key/value pairs, and a session context, into a proper TripDescription-Record.

```
validateTripDescription :: Params → SessionContext → Maybe TripDescriptionRecord
validateTripDescription ps (graph, session) =
    let
        originCity' = validateCity graph $ valueForParam "originCity" ps
        destinationCity' = validateCity graph $ valueForParam "destinationCity" ps
        dateOfDeparture' = fromJust . validateDate $ valueForParam "dateOfDeparture" ps
        dateOfReturn' = (lookup "dateOfReturn" ps) >>= validateDate
        maxTotalPrice' = (lookup "maxTotalPrice" ps) >>= read
        maxTotalDuration' = (lookup "maxTotalDuration" ps) >>= read
        sortingPreference' = case fromJust $ lookup "sortingPreference" ps of
                    "SortByPrice" → SortByPrice
                    "SortByDuration" → SortByDuration
    in
        if (isJust originCity') && (isJust destinationCity')
        then
            Just TripDescriptionRecord
            { originCity = fromJust originCity'
            , destinationCity = fromJust destinationCity'
            , dateOfDeparture = dateOfDeparture'
            , dateOfReturn = dateOfReturn'
            , maxTotalPrice = maxTotalPrice'
            , maxTotalDuration = maxTotalDuration'
            , sortingPreference = sortingPreference'
            }
        else Nothing
```

The function needs access to the graph inside the session context because it must query the graph for the list of existing cities. It returns **Nothing** when either the origin city or the destination city cannot be found in the graph. Note that this case should not occur in practice, because the *input* to this validation function will be data from a form that lets the customer *pick* one city from a given list of all available cities. An erroneous situation can only happen when the HTTP query string has been tampered with.

The function is used in the TripList page before the data is passed on to the functions checkWellformedness and prepareTripList. The defining function for that page is tasTripList, of which the interesting code fragments are given below:

```
tasTripList :: StatefulPageFunc
tasTripList params = do
    (graph, session) ← get
```

```
    navigation ← tasNavigation params
    tripDescr ← return $ validateTripDescription params (graph, session)
    if (isJust tripDescr && checkWellformedness (fromJust tripDescr))
        then do
            trips ← return $ prepareTrips (fromJust tripDescr) (graph, session)
            (newgraph, tripDescrNode) ← return $ storeTrips trips graph
            put (newgraph, setValue session "tripDescription" (show tripDescrNode))
            return $ tasMainTemplate (Element "slots" [])
                -- ...
        else
            tasTripDescription params
```

Here we can also see that the page updates the internal state by adding nodes to the graph (via addTripDescription) and by storing a reference to a trip description node in the session dictionary.

The page functions rely on the following functions that encapsulate the actual querying. The query functions will be defined in section 11.8.

```
-- | returns a customer's method preferences
getMethodPrefs :: AttributedGraph → String → [String]
getMethodPrefs = queryMethodPrefsForCustomer

-- | returns a list of all cities
getAllCities :: AttributedGraph → [String]
getAllCities = queryAllCities

-- | returns a list of /all/ cities
getOriginCities :: AttributedGraph → [String]
getOriginCities = getAllCities

-- | returns a list of /all/ cities
getDestCities :: AttributedGraph → [String]
getDestCities = getAllCities
```

As a matter of fact, the functions do not provide any additional features apart from wrapping the actual calls to the query functions. They are important nevertheless, because they introduce a new vocabulary to refer to graph queries. The function getOriginCities, for example, is defined to be the same as getAllCities, instead of directly using a query that retrieves all cities. This allows to introduce an intermediate level of abstraction that could be exploited towards page function definitions that are easier to read and thus easier to maintain. Admittedly, the examples given above are not complex enough to really show off this feature, but the pattern should shine through anyhow.

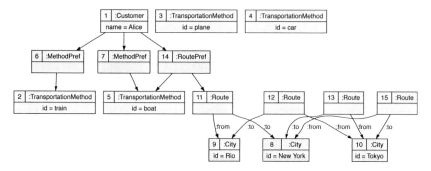

Figure 11.4: The example instance graph for the TAS (syntax: see text)

11.7 Graph representation

For demonstration purposes, the data is stored in a graph that is represented as a Haskell data structure, using the Functional Graph Library (FGL). In general, storing and accessing the instance data could be performed via *any* means, provided that it has a functional interface. The alternative discussed here suggests itself because of its coherency and adequate simplicity.

A small example instance graph is depicted in figure 11.4. The diagram was automatically created from the Haskell representation, in the same way as this was achieved for the Computer Science Faculty instance data (see section 6.1.1, which also contains the definition of the syntax used). The graph *complies* to the content model described in section 11.2 insofar as nodes and edges of the graph represent instances of classes and associations, respectively. In other words, the class diagram in figure 11.2 represents a valid *schema* for that graph.

The Haskell code necessary to build the graph was sketched in section 3.4.2. For the queries, we will rely on the auxiliary functions defined and described in section 3.4.

11.8 Queries

This section defines the queries necessary for the page functions. According to the discipline introduced for the page functions, only selected queries will be briefly discussed here. In order to show how the queries could look like, we will employ the functions introduced in section 3.4.3 because they are compatible with the graph implementation used. Since the page functions abstract from the actual implementation of the queries, the graph representation as well as the graph query language are freely exchangeable. Note that graph *updates* are performed by the page functions, for example tasTripList.

The function queryAllCities returns the names of all cities.

```
queryAllCities :: AttributedGraph → [String]
queryAllCities g =
   nodesToValues
      g
      (λ lbl → getValue lbl "id")
      (query g (nodes g) [ constrainByType "City" ])
```

The function nodes (from the FGL) returns a list of *all* nodes of the given graph. With the help of nodesToValues, the actual city names, stored in the attribute id, are extracted from the nodes that are returned by query.

The function queryAllTransportationMethods can be used to get a list of all possible transportation methods. It is defined as:

```
queryAllTransportationMethods :: AttributedGraph → [String]
queryAllTransportationMethods g =
   nodesToValues
      g
      (λ lbl → getValue lbl "id")
      (query g (nodes g) [ constrainByType "TransportationMethod" ])
```

The function queryMethodPrefsForCustomer returns a list of all preferred transportation methods for a given customer c. The argument c is the customer's name.

```
queryMethodPrefsForCustomer :: AttributedGraph → String → [String]
queryMethodPrefsForCustomer g c =
   nodesToValues
      g
      (λ lbl → getValue lbl "id")
      (query
         g
         (nodes g)
         [ constrainByType "Customer"
         , constrainByAttr "name" c
         , suc
         , constrainByType "MethodPref"
         , suc
         , constrainByType "TransportationMethod"
         ]
      )
```

11.9 Presentation

The conversion of the pages into a language that can be rendered by a web browser is achieved by specifying a translation from the abstract page description into XHTML. Since we have been using the same APD element instances as for the computer science faculty web site, we can resort to the functions defined in chapter 10.

Part III

Conclusion

Summary

This work shows that the *combination* of web site modelling and functional specification is a powerful tool for defining what a web site should consist of.

We build upon many ideas that have been developed over the years. The field of *web engineering*, a label that nicely fits to the way of thinking that we feel committed to, has emerged from a plethora of separate directions of scientific work and is on its way to consolidate to a proper discipline, akin to *software engineering*. As the subject for our work, we chose to look into model-driven approaches for web site generation *and* functional programming languages as a means for formal specification. Studying the available publications from both 'fields' disclosed many ideas and inspirational sources. The chapter on related work hopefully succeeded in summarising these findings.

For the convenience of the reader, the introductory part of this work is completed by a summary of the concepts of the Haskell language. This functional programming language is used as an example language throughout the text,

Thus, there is a fundament, capable of bearing what we built on top of it. The identification of a set of six separate concerns led to the definition of six types of models that are integrated and, taken together, accurately describe a web site. The concerns one has to account for are:

- the content of the web site, given as a conceptualisation of the application domain and corresponding instance data;
- queries and update functions that access the data and that can be used to abstract from its fine-grained structure;
- the dynamics of the web site, also called the business logic;
- the composition of web pages, the building blocks for the web site;
- the navigation structure of the web site; and
- the presentation of the web pages for a given output medium.

Each concern, and each respective model, has a separate chapter devoted to it. The integration of the models is facilitated by the coherence of their definitions. The queries, updates, dynamics, pages, and the presentation are all defined by means of *functions*.

But not only does this ease the integration, it also opens many possibilities for the introduction of additional abstraction levels. The most important advantage of employing a functional programming language for these specification is, however, the huge amount of flexibility. On any conceivable level, one can exploit the expressive power of the declarative language.

The remaining models, i.e., the content model and the navigation structure, are treated in the 'traditional' way. There was nothing to gain in leaving well-trodden paths at this point.

The ideas are presented both abstractly and by means of two examples, showing that the findings are indeed applicable. In the course of the introduction of the models, we refer to the Computer Science Faculty web site of the Koblenz-Landau University. The second example, a travel agency system, is dealt with in one single chapter, which makes it easy to follow the necessary steps.

Outlook

It would be a grand achievement if one could rightfully claim at this point that this work had covered every aspect one could think of, and that there were no further topics worth considering. However, this is not the case. Although the approach described herein is consistent and complete, it marks the starting point rather than the ultimate end of the journey towards the 'one and only' way to model and create web sites.

As was already pointed out, the approach is inherently open and flexible. We tried to refrain from making any decision that would have constrained the openness in any way. Thus, future extensions and alterations are facilitated and even encouraged.

We are aware of the fact that the specifications that are to be delivered for the modelling of a web site are proper functional programs. As such, they are rather concise, high-level, well-typed, and syntactically clean. At the same time, their creation and maintenance is everything *but* convenient for a person who has no experience in functional programming. Although a functional language is quite easy to learn (as the author can confirm from his own experience), using them for the specification of web sites is not the medium of choice for non-computer scientists. Of course, this had not been our intent in the first place, but, in order to provide more comfort, using a software tool that aids in the creation of the specifications might be beneficial. We envision that the functional specifications are automatically created, rather than crafted manually.

During the description of the querying and update functions, it became apparent that the graph model used in the actual implementation provided room for improvements. It would have been significantly easier to define queries for proper TGraphs, particularly when using a 'real' query language like GReQL ([Kam98]). In principle, the substitution is possible and should not pose any difficulties. The same holds for the integration of other data repositories, like relational databases.

It is encouraging and thrilling to think about these possible extensions and further steps of improvement. Looking forward is as important as looking back; but not moving on means staying behind.

Part IV

Appendix

Executable Web Page Specifications

This chapter relates on the integration of the web site specification into the run-time environment, making the specification executable. The integration was achieved by interfacing the Haskell interpreter *Hugs* ([OGI04]) from the platform used to actually run the web site (i.e., *Zope*). The end result of this effort is a system that is able to directly execute a given functional specification of a web site. Changes to the specification are effective immediately, because the specification is re-interpreted every time a request for a web page is made. This also allows to effortlessly support dynamic and virtual web pages.

14.1 Technical Foundations

The interaction between a web client and the system delivering the web pages follows a simple request/response pattern, defined by the hypertext transfer protocol (HTTP): a request for a web resource (identified by a URL) is passed to the web server, which responds with either the content of the resource or an error message. The request sent to the server may contain parameters, coded as key/value-pairs. These parameters, together with the URL, are used by the web server to determine which page to deliver. In order to produce pages dynamically, the parameters are typically passed to a separate process started by the web server that handles the actual calculation of the page content (CGI).

In the context of pages that are APD structures produced by functions, the interaction can be described by the following steps, performed cyclically:

1. A request containing an URL and a (possibly empty) set of parameters is received by the web server.

2. The web server determines the page function identified by this request (both, the URL and the parameters, may influence this decision).

3. The web server evaluates the page function, using the parameters from the request. The evaluation yields an APD structure.

4. The web server transforms the APD structure into the chosen output format (notably, XHTML).

5. The web server emits the output, returns it to the client, and awaits the next request.

The term 'web server' refers to a complex module whose inner structure is irrelevant at this point. The different steps will most probably be performed by dedicated units inside the web server.

Some of the points require further explanation, which shall be given in the following sections.

Receiving a Request

The client sends an HTTP request to the web server. This request contains all information necessary to specify the resource the client wants to receive (HTTP GET) or the action the client wants the server to perform (HTTP POST). The web server receives the request, analyses it and triggers appropriate actions.

In addition to what HTTP provides, the web server should perform some 'convenience' functions, like maintaining a session object that can be used during page generation. The state represented by the session object is automatically preserved across different HTTP requests. The state normally comprises a set of variables that are needed in the page functions. It could also contain the notion of the *current page node* that may help to implement the navigation.

Determining the Page Function

The request must uniquely identify a page function that can be evaluated to generate an APD structure. Therefore, a mapping is needed that defines which combination of URL and parameters maps to which page function.

The URL can be regarded as a path expression that identifies a page along the path in the primary navigation structure. The last component of the URL may be the first parameter to a virtual page, which in turn is identified by the last but one component. In order to pick the page that corresponds to a given URL, one starts at the site root and descends the tree defined by the primary navigation structure along the path that is coded in the URL (from left to right), consuming one path component at a time. Thus, eventually, the page is reached. Should there be remaining path components in the URL, they are defined to be parameters to the page that are simply passed to it along with the other parameters contained in the request.

In principle, this algorithm could be replaced by the application of a hash table that directly maps URLs to pages. Or, in other words, each page could be equipped with an identifier that is the (unique) position of this page in the primary navigation structure.

Before the actual page node is picked, a wrapper function could check whether the client is authorised to access the page in question. This requires the client to send authentication data along with the HTTP request that can be used to identify the client and to map this identity to a permission scheme.

Evaluating the Page Function

Once the page node is available, the whole page can be produced by evaluating the page function. Parameters passed in are used as needed.

Evaluating a page function may produce errors if necessary parameters are not given. These errors must be handled properly and returned to the client.

Generating HTML

Conversion from a given APD structure into the appropriate output format is done by the presentation function as the last step prior to sending the result to the client. In this section, we focus on generating (X)HTML, but any other XML language can be used as well (see section 10.1).

An APD structure can be traversed by a conversion function that defines how elements are to be transformed into HTML. As far as Element nodes, Text nodes, and Field nodes are concerned, this transformation is straightforward. However, links and forms deserve a more detailed look, because they contain function calls. Section 10.3 already gave a description of the necessary transformation steps.

Sending the result

In the final step, the generated result is sent back to the client that initiated the request. The result gets packed into an HTTP response.

14.2 Making Zope aware of Haskell

In order to provide the executable specification, Zope is used as an HTTP server that effectively calls an Haskell interpreter to evaluate Haskell functions. The function identifier and parameters are passed via the URL, and the function returns HTML code that is passed back to the client where the HTTP request originated from.

The following section defines the interface between Zope and Hugs, the Haskell interpreter.

Haskell Side

On the Haskell side, there is no need for any special provisions. The Haskell functions that are to be called via the web server have to return a string that is a valid HTML document. Parameters to the functions are passed as a list of key/value tuples (type [(String, String)]).

The page functions are of the type PageFunc, which is defined to be a mapping of a parameter list to an APD. The APD is converted to XHTML with the help of two conversion functions: linksToHTMLElements and showXML.

The function linksToHTMLElements was defined as

```
linksToHTMLElements :: APD → (Identifier → String) → APD
linksToHTMLElements n@(Text s) _ = n
linksToHTMLElements (Element n a es) id2url =
    Element n a (map (λe → linksToHTMLElements e id2url) es)
linksToHTMLElements (Link n a es pid pa) id2url =
    Element "a" ([ ("href", (id2url pid)++(paramsToURI pa)) ] ++ a) es
linksToHTMLElements (Form n a es pid pa) id2url =
    Element "form"
      (
        [ ("name", n)
        , ("method", "post")
        , ("action", (id2url pid)++(paramsToURI pa))
        ]
        ++ a
      )
      (map (λe → linksToHTMLElements e id2url) es)
linksToHTMLElements (Field n a s) id2url =
    Element "input"
      ( [ ("name", n) ] ++ a )
      [Text s]
linksToHTMLElements x _ = x −−−Empty
```

It converts one APD structure into another one by replacing Link, Form and Field nodes with normal Element nodes, so that the resulting APD structure can be directly transformed into an HTML representation. Link nodes are replaced by "a" anchor elements, Form nodes are replaced by "form" elements, and Field nodes are replaced by "input" elements. Links and forms are equipped with a destination URL, which is calculated by calling the function that was passed to linksToHTMLElements as its second parameter. This function should create a valid URL from a given function identifier.

The linksToHTMLElements function utilises the helper function paramsToURI, which constructs an URI conform string from a list of parameters.

```
paramsToURI :: Params → String
paramsToURI [] = ""
paramsToURI ps = foldl (++) "?" (
    map (λ(k,v) → k ++ "=" ++ v) ps )
```

The function showXML converts an APD to an XML string. It invests some effort to produce a 'nice looking' XML representation by indenting the lines according to the depth of the element nesting. The conversion itself, however, is straight forward with two exceptions: Link and Form nodes, which have a more complex structure as would be directly mappable to one XML element. Therefore, a nested element is created for each of them. This feature, however, is not necessary for the setting where showXML is used in this text, since all Link and Form nodes have already been converted to normal Element nodes by linksToHTMLElements.

```
showXML :: APD → String
showXML a = showXML' 0 a
  where
    showXML' :: Int → APD → String
    showXML' l (Text s) = (indent l) ++ (s) ++ "\n"
    showXML' l (Element n a es) =
      (indent l) ++ "<" ++ (n) ++ (showAttrs a) ++ ">\n"
        ++ (foldr (++) [] (map (showXML' (l+1)) es))
        ++ (indent l) ++ "</" ++ (n) ++ ">\n"
    showXML' l (Link n a es pid pa) =
      (indent l) ++ "<link␣id="
        ++ (show n) ++ (showAttrs a) ++ ">\n"
        ++ (indent (l+1)) ++ "<destpage␣pageid=" ++ (show pid)
        ++ (showAttrs pa) ++ "/>\n"
        ++ (indent (l+1)) ++ "<text>\n"
        ++ (foldr (++) [] (map (showXML' (l+2)) es))
        ++ (indent (l+1)) ++ "</text>\n"
        ++ (indent l) ++ "</link>\n"
    showXML' l (Form n a es pid pa) =
      (indent l) ++ "<form␣name=" ++ (n) ++ (showAttrs a) ++ ">\n"
        ++ (indent (l+1)) ++ "<destpage␣pageid=" ++ (show pid)
        ++ (showAttrs pa) ++ "/>\n"
        ++ (indent (l+1)) ++ "<text>\n"
        ++ (foldr (++) [] (map (showXML' (l+2)) es))
        ++ (indent (l+1)) ++ "</text>\n"
        ++ (indent l) ++ "</form>\n"
    showXML' l (Field n a es s) =
      (indent l) ++ "<field␣name=" ++ (show n) ++ (showAttrs a) ++ ">\n"
        ++ (indent (l+1)) ++ "<value>" ++ s ++ "</value>\n"
        ++ (foldr (++) [] (map (showXML' (l+2)) es))
        ++ (indent l) ++ "</field>\n"
    showXML' l Empty =
      (indent l) ++ "<Empty/>"

    indent :: Int → String
    indent i = replicate (i*2) ' '

    showAttrs :: Attrs → String
    showAttrs ((ak,av):as) =
      "␣" ++ ak ++ "=" ++ (show av) ++ (showAttrs as)
    showAttrs [] = ""
```

Zope Side

On the Zope side, the Python script "run" is responsible to accept calls from the web client and to return the result of evaluating the requested Haskell function.

```
code='''
:load␣"/Applications/Eclipse/workspace/WebSites/src/Definitions.hs"
:load␣"/Applications/Eclipse/workspace/WebSites/src/FB4PageFuncs.hs"
putStr␣""
putStr␣(showXML␣(linksToHTMLElements␣(%s␣%s)␣resourceURL))
'''

pageFuncId = traverse_subpath[0]
paramsKeys = container.REQUEST.form.keys()
params = map(
    lambda key: '("%s","%s")' % (key, container.REQUEST.form[key]),
    paramsKeys )
params = "[" + ",".join(params) + "]"

code = code % (pageFuncId, params)

return container.execHaskellCode(code, 'FB4PageFuncs')
```

The script consults the URI it was called with. In Zope, the parts of this URI are accessible via an API. A possible call might look like this:

http://...path.../run/fb4NewsItem?id=news_00079

The path to the folder that contains the run script has been omitted. Everything behind run/ is considered a parameter to the script. There are two kinds of parameters: *path components* and *query strings*.

Path components are written as slash-separated identifiers. The list of path components ends at a question mark or at the end of the string. In the example above, the string fb4NewsItem is the only path component. To the caller of the web page, the path components look like normal folders (every component but the last) or files (the last component). It is not directly apparent that run is the name of a script. This technique allows us to cloak the fact that the web pages do not really exist as objects, but are dynamically calculated by parameterising the run script.

Query strings are key/value pairs. The list of query strings is introduced by a question mark. One key and the associated value are separated by an equals sign, the pairs are separated by ampersand signs (the example above contains only one pair).

The script treats the path component parameter (there must be only one) as the identifier of a Haskell function. The query strings are treated as parameters to this function. Using these pieces of information, the script constructs a string that contains valid Hugs code. This code is passed to a Hugs interpreter (via the standard input) and the result (via the standard output) is read, stripped[1], and returned to the caller.

The code passed to Hugs is the following:

_____

[1] Hugs produces some amount of status information that we have to get rid of.

```
:load "/Applications/Eclipse/workspace/WebSites/src/Definitions.hs"
:load "/Applications/Eclipse/workspace/WebSites/src/FB4PageFuncs.hs"
putStr ""
putStr (showXML (linksToHTMLElements (%s %s) resourceURL))
```

The first two statements load the necessary modules (the generic definitions, like the
APD type, as well as the web page functions for the example web site). The last two lines
are two expressions that produce an empty line and the actual HTML output. The two
'%s's are replaced with the function identifier and the parameters, respectively.

For our example, the last line actually passed to Hugs would be

```
putStr (showXML (linksToHTMLElements
   (fb4NewsItem [("id","news_00079")]) resourceURL))
```

The line-break has been inserted manually to improve legibility.

One can see that the function resourceURL is passed to linksToHTMLElements as a conversion
function to create valid URLs from resource identifiers (i.e., identifiers of web pages and
images). In our example, it is defined as

```
resourceURL :: Identifier → String
resourceURL "currentPhoto" = (baseURL ++ "/../Layout/Images/photo.jpg")
resourceURL other = (baseURL ++ "/" ++ other)

baseURL :: String
baseURL = "."
```

It is important to note that it is possible to construct *any* valid Haskell code and pass it
to the interpreter. This is especially useful for passing along parameters that are not
coded in the URI, which is absolutely necessary when the functions shall be able to
access context information like session variables, authorisation information or other data
that is provided by the run-time system. Thus, when evaluating Haskell functions, we do
not have to rely on what is given in one URI, but we can consider state information as
well.

Definitions

This section lists important relevant terms used in this text and gives definitions for them. It is tried to keep them as brief and precise as possible. Some of the definitions are also included in the main text, but they will be repeated here for convenience.

artefact   An *artefact* is an object that is made by a person.

aspect   In computer science, the term *aspect* has different connotations, and it has a special meaning in the context of *aspect orientation* (one possible definition being 'the combination of a point-cut and an advice'). In this text, however, the term is not used with this specific meaning unless stated otherwise. Rather, we refer to the common meaning, 'a particular part or feature of a situation, an idea, or a problem'.

authorisation   The term *authorisation* is the act of ensuring that a given web site visitor has the permission to perform a certain task. See section 4.3.

breadcrumbs   Breadcrumb navigation displays the current page's context within the site structure. The term *breadcrumb* is as in 'Hänsel and Gretel' – leaving a trail of crumbs in order to find their way back out of the forest. Showing the context explicitly greatly helps to avoid the effect of 'getting lost' (cf. [Con87]).

customisation   *Customisation* is defined to be the 'adaptation of an application's services towards its context' [KPRS03, p. 82].

FB4   *FB4* is an abbreviation for 'Fachbereich 4', which means 'faculty 4' in English. Faculty number four of the Koblenz-Landau University is the computer science faculty, whose web site was chosen as an example in this text (see section 4.4).

functional   As pointed out in section 1.1, the adjective *functional* has four different meanings: (1) practical and useful; with little or no decoration; (2) having a special purpose; making it possible for somebody to do something or for something to happen (3) working, or able to work; (4) involving mathematical functions.

model   A *model* is a 'simplified description of a system used in explanations, calculations, etc.' [Hor89, model (n) 3] A model is an abstraction that is precise enough to describe what the desired result should comprise of.

permission   A *permission* defines *what* can be done with a particular object.

resource   A *resource* is 'anything that has identity' ([BLFIM98])

role   A *role* in the context of authorisation is a collection of visitors.

user agent   A *user agent* is the "client which initiates a request. These are often browsers, editors, spiders (web-traversing robots), or other end user tools" http://www.ietf.org/rfc/rfc2616.txt.

visitor   A *visitor* is a person experiencing a *web site*⋄ by looking at its rendered version and using the functionality provided by it. That basically means following the hyperlinks and thus calling for further *web page*⋄ to be loaded. A visitor can also be a piece of software acting in like manner. See also section 4.3.

Web   The term *Web*, written with a capital 'W', is short for the World Wide Web (WWW).

web engineering   The *web engineering* discipline is obliged to 'the application of systematic, disciplined and quantifiable approaches to the cost-effective development, operation, and evolution of high-quality applications in the World Wide Web.' [Web05]

web page   A *web page* is one distinguished *resource*⋄ in a *web site*⋄. If one wants to emphasise that a web page is a part of *the* Web, one writes Web page (capital 'W') rather than web page.

web service   A *web service* is a programmatic interface to an application that can be addressed over the Internet (http://www.w3.org/2002/ws/) using well-defined protocols. The interface can be used by another application to connect to the service, request an operation be performed, and receive a message containing the result. All communication is sent as XML documents.

'A Web service is a software system identified by a URI ([BLFIM98]), whose public interfaces and bindings are defined and described using XML. Its definition can be discovered by other software systems. These systems may then interact with the Web service in a manner prescribed by its definition, using XML based messages conveyed by Internet protocols.' [http://www.w3.org/TR/wsa-reqs]

web site   A *web site* is a coherent and related collection of *resources*⋄, typically including one distinguished resource (home page) acting as an entry point into the collection. The term *web presence* is sometimes used synonymous to web site.

Bibliography

[AAB⁺05]   Conny Andersson, Martin Andersson, Mary Bergman, Victor Blomqvist, Björn Bringert, Anders Höckersten, and Torbjörn Martin. HaskellDB. http://haskelldb.sourceforge.net/, May 2005.

[Abb83]   Russel J. Abbott. Program design by informal english descriptions. *Commun. ACM*, 26(11):882–894, 1983.

[Aum05]   David Aumueller. Beer ontology. http://www.schemaweb.info/schema/SchemaDetails.aspx?id=99, July 2005.

[Bec00]   Kent Beck. *Extreme programming explained: embrace change.* Addison-Wesley Longman Publishing Co., Inc., Boston, MA, USA, 2000.

[Ben05]   Jim Bender. Reading list on XML and web programming. http://readscheme.org/xml-web/, May 2005.

[BGL98]   Michael Bieber, Roberto Galnares, and Qiang Lu. Web engineering and flexible hypermedia. In Peter Brusilovksy and Paul de Bra, editors, *Proceedings of the 2nd Workshop on Adaptive Hypertext and Hypermedia (Hypertext 98)*, Pittsburgh, USA, June 1998.

[BHA⁺04]   Björn Bringert, Anders Höckersten, Conny Andersson, Martin Andersson, Mary Bergman, Victor Blomqvist, and Torbjörn Martin. Student paper: HaskellDB improved. In *Haskell '04: Proceedings of the ACM SIGPLAN workshop on Haskell*, pages 108–115. ACM Press, 2004.

[BL89]   Tim Berners-Lee. Information management: A proposal. http://www.w3.org/History/1989/proposal.html, March 1989.

[BL99]   Tim Berners-Lee. *Weaving the Web: The Original Design and Ultimate Destiny of the World Wide Web by Its Inventor.* Harper San Francisco, 1999.

[BLFIM98]   T. Berners-Lee, R. Fielding, U.C. Irvine, and L. Masinter. RFC 2396: Uniform Resource Identifiers (URI): Generic Syntax. http://www.ietf.org/rfc/rfc2396.txt, 1998.

[BM04]   John Boyer and Roland Merrick. XForms 1.1 Requirements. W3C Working Group Note, http://www.w3.org/TR/xforms-11-req/, August 2004.

[BMS02]   Claus Brabrand, Anders Møller, and Michael I. Schwartzbach. The <bigwig> project. *ACM Transactions on Internet Technology*, 2(2):79–114, 2002.

[Bus45]   Vannevar Bush. As We May Think. *The Atlantic Monthly*, 176(1):101–108, 1945.

[CFB+03]   Stefano Ceri, Piero Fraternali, Aldo Bongio, Marco Brambilla, Sara Comai, and Maristella Matera. *Designing Data-Intensive Web Applications*. Morgan Kaufmann Publishers, Inc., San Francisco, CA, USA, 2003.

[Cla99]   James Clark. XSL Transformations (XSLT) Version 1.0. W3C Recommendation, http://www.w3.org/TR/xslt, 1999.

[Con87]   Jeff Conklin. Hypertext: An Introduction and Survey. *IEEE Computer*, 20(9):17–41, 1987.

[Con99]   Jim Conallen. Modeling Web application architectures with UML. *Communications of the ACM*, 42(10):63–70, 1999.

[Coo05]   Andrew Cooke. Halipeto. http://acooke.org/jara/halipeto/, May 2005.

[DEF+98]   Peter Dahm, Jürgen Ebert, Angelika Franzke, Manfred Kamp, and Andreas Winter. TGraphen und EER-Schemata - formale Grundlagen. In Ebert et al. [EGSW98].

[DL98]   O. M. F. De Troyer and C. J. Leune. WSDM: a user centered design method for Web sites. *Computer Networks and ISDN Systems (1985–1998)*, 30(1–7):85–94, 1998.

[Dot05]   The DOT language. http://www.graphviz.org/cvs/doc/info/lang.html, 2005.

[EGSW98]   Jürgen Ebert, Rainer Gimnich, Hans H. Stasch, and Andreas Winter, editors. *GUPRO–Generische Umgebung zum Programmverstehen*. Fölbach, Koblenz, 1998.

[EN05]   John Ellson and Stephen North. Graphviz – graph drawing software. http://www.graphviz.org, 2005.

[Erw01]   Martin Erwig. Inductive graphs and functional graph algorithms. *Journal of Functional Programming*, 11(5):467–492, 2001.

[EWD+96]   Jürgen Ebert, Andreas Winter, Peter Dahm, Angelika Franzke, and Roger Süttenbach. Graph based modeling and implementation with EER/GRAL. In B. Thalheim, editor, *15th International Conference on Conceptual Modeling (ER'96), Proceedings*, number 1157 in LNCS, pages 163–178, Berlin, 1996. Springer.

[FFLS00]   Mary Fernández, Daniela Florescu, Alon Y. Levy, and Dan Suciu. Declarative specification of Web sites with Strudel. *VLDB Journal*, 9(1):38–55, 2000.

[Fra99]   Piero Fraternali. Tools and approaches for developing data-intensive Web applications: a survey. *ACM Computing Surveys*, 31(3):227–263, 1999.

[FST99]   Mary Fernández, Dan Suciu, and Igor Tatarinov. Declarative specification of data-intensive web sites. In *Domain-Specific Languages*, pages 135–148, 1999.

[Gar03]   Jesse James Garrett. *The Elements of User Experience: User-Centered Design for the Web*. New Riders, Indianapolis, Indiana, 2003.

[GC00]   D. Germán and D. Cowan. Towards a unified catalog of hypermedia design patterns. *Proc. 33rd Hawaii International Conference on System Science*, 2000.

[GCP00]   Jaime Gómez, Cristina Cachero, and Oscar Pastor. Extending a conceptual modelling approach to web application design. In *Conference on Advanced Information Systems Engineering*, pages 79–93, 2000.

[GHJV94]   E. Gamma, R. Helm, R. Johnson, and J. Vlissides. *Design Patterns – Elements of Reusable Object-Oriented Software*. Addison-Wesley, 1994.

[GN87]   Michael R. Genesereth and Nils J. Nilsson. *Logical Foundations of Artificial Intelligence*. Morgan Kaufmann Publishers Inc., San Francisco, CA, USA, 1987.

[GN02]   Ekaterina Gorshkova and Boris Novikov. Exploiting UML extensibility in the design of web information systems. In *Proc. Fifth International Baltic Conference on Databases and Information Systems*, pages 49–64, Tallinn, Estonia, June 2002.

[GPS93]   Franca Garzotto, Paolo Paolini, and Daniel Schwabe. HDM – a model-based approach to hypertext application design. *ACM Transactions on Information Systems*, 11(1):1–26, 1993.

[HK99]   Martin Hitz and Gerti Kappel. *UML@Work. Von der Analyse zur Realisierung*. dpunkt.verlag, Heidelberg, 1999.

[HK01]   Rolf Hennicker and Nora Koch. Modeling the user interface of web applications with UML. In Andy Evans, Robert B. France, Ana M. D. Moreira, and Bernhard Rumpe, editors, *pUML*, volume 7 of *LNI*, pages 158–172. GI, 2001.

[Hoa62]   Charles Antony Richard Hoare. Quicksort. *The Computer Journal*, 5(1):10–16, 1962.

[Hor89]   A S Hornby, editor. *Oxford Advanced Learner's Dictionary of Current English*. Oxford University Press, Walton Street, Oxford OX2 6DP, fourth edition, 1989.

[HPF99]   Paul Hudak, John Peterson, and Joseph Fasel. Gentle Introduction To Haskell, version 98. http://haskell.org/tutorial, 1999.

[ISB95]   Tomás Isakowitz, Edward A. Stohr, and P. Balasubramanian. RMM: A methodology for structured hypermedia design. *Communications of the ACM*, 38(8):34–44, 1995.

[Jac05]   Alex Jacobson. HAppS. http://happs.org/, August 2005.

[JGF96]   Simon Peter Jones, Andrew Gordon, and Sigbjorn Finne. Concurrent Haskell. In *Conference Record of POPL '96: The 23rd ACM SIGPLAN-SIGACT Symposium on Principles of Programming Languages*, pages 295–308, St. Petersburg Beach, Florida, Jan 1996. ACM Press.

[JH98]   Simon Peyton Jones and John Hughes. The Haskell 98 Report. http://haskell.org/definition, as of 2005-02-09, 1998.

[Kam98]   Manfred Kamp. GReQL - eine Anfragesprache für das GUPRO-Repository 1.1. In Ebert et al. [EGSW98], pages 173–202.

[KKH01]   Nora Koch, Andreas Kraus, and Rolf Hennicker. The authoring process of the UML-based Web engineering approach. http://www.dsic.upv.es/~west/iwwost01/files/contributions/NoraKoch/Uwe.pdf, June 2001. (on-line).

[Koc99]   Nora Koch. A comparative study of methods for hypermedia development. Technical Report 9905, Ludwig Maximilians-Universität München, November 1999.

[KPRR04]   Gerti Kappel, Birgit Pröll, Siegfried Reich, and Werner Retschitzegger, editors. *Web Engineering: Systematische Entwicklung von Web-Anwendungen.* dpunkt.verlag, Heidelberg, 2004.

[KPRS03]   Gerti Kappel, Birgit Pröll, Werner Retschitzegger, and Wieland Schwinger. Customisation for ubiquitous web applications – A comparison of approaches. *International Journal of Web Engineering Technology*, 1(1):79–111, 2003.

[KRS00]   Gerti Kappel, Werner Retschitzegger, and Wieland Schwinger. Modeling customizable Web applications – a requirement's perspective. In *Kyoto International Conference on Digital Libraries*, page 387, 2000.

[Kru00]   Philippe Kruchten. *The Rational Unified Process: An Introduction, Second Edition.* Addison-Wesley Longman Publishing Co., Inc., Boston, MA, USA, 2000.

[Lan96]   Danny B. Lange. An object-oriented design approach for developing hypermedia information systems. *J. Organ. Comput. Electron. Commer.*, 6(3):269–293, 1996.

[Lei03]   Daniel Johannes Pieter Leijen. *The λ Abroad – A Functional Approach to Software Components.* PhD thesis, Department of Computer Science, Universiteit Utrecht, The Netherlands, November 2003.

[Lei05]   Daan Leijen. HaskellDB. http://www.haskell.org/haskellDB/, May 2005.

[LH99]   David Lowe and Wendy Hall. *Hypermedia and the Web: An Engineering Approach.* John Wiley and Sons, 1999.

[LHYT00]   Karl R.P.H. Leung, Lucas C.K. Hui, S.M. Yiu, and Ricky W.M. Tang. Modelling Web Navigation by Statechart. In *24th International Computer Software and Applications Conference (COMPSAC 2000), 25-28 October 2000, Taipei, Taiwan*, pages 41–47. IEEE Computer Society, 2000.

[LLY98]   Heeseok Lee, Choongseok Lee, and Cheonsoo Yoo. A scenario-based object-oriented methodology for developing hypermedia information systems. In *HICSS (2)*, pages 47–, 1998.

[LM99]   Daan Leijen and Erik Meijer. Domain-specific embedded compilers. In *Proceedings of The 2nd Conference on Domain-Specific Languages*, Austin, Texas, USA, Oct 1999. Usenix.

[Mar02]   Simon Marlow. Developing a high-performance web server in Concurrent Haskell. *Journal of Functional Programming*, 12(4+5):359–374, July 2002.

[Mar05]   Simon Marlow. The Glasgow Haskell Compiler. http://www.haskell.org/ghc/, August 2005.

[MC05]   Anders Møller and Aske Simon Christensen. JWIG. http://www.brics.dk/JWIG/, May 2005.

[Mil05]   Eric Miller. Semantic web activity statement. http://www.w3.org/2001/sw/Activity.html, July 2005.

[MMCF03]   Maristella Matera, Andrea Maurino, Stefano Ceri, and Piero Fraternali. Model-driven design of collaborative web applications. *Softw. Pract. Exper.*, 33(8):701–732, 2003.

[MW05]   Merriam-Webster. Merriam-Webster Online. http://www.m-w.com/cgi-bin/dictionary, July 2005.

[New05]   Jeff Newbern. All about monads. A comprehensive guide to the theory and practice of monadic programming in Haskell. http://www.nomaware.com/monads, as of 2005-03-03, 2005.

[NN95]   Jocelyne Nanard and Marc Nanard. Hypertext design environments and the hypertext design process. *Commun. ACM*, 38(8):49–56, 1995.

[Nør05]   Kurt Nørmark. Web programming in Scheme with LAML. *Journal of Functional Programming*, 15(1):53–65, Jan 2005.

[NP01]   Ian Niles and Adam Pease. Towards a standard upper ontology. In *FOIS '01: Proceedings of the international conference on Formal Ontology in Information Systems*, pages 2–9, New York, NY, USA, 2001. ACM Press.

[OGI04]   OGI and Yale. Hugs 98 Web Site. http://www.haskell.org/hugs/, August 2004.

[Oxf05]   Oxford. Oxford advanced learner's dictionary (online). http://www.oup.
           com/oald-bin/web_getald7index1a.pl, July 2005.

[PC04]   John Peterson and Olaf Chitil. The Haskell Home Page. http://www.haskell.
           org/, Dec 2004.

[RM02]   Louis Rosenfeld and Peter Morville. *Information Architecture for the World
           Wide Web*. O'Reilly & Associates, Inc., Sebastopol, CA, USA, 2002.

[RS00]   Werner Retschitzegger and Wieland Schwinger. Towards modeling of
           dataweb applications – a requirements' perspective. In *Proc. of the Americas
           Conference on Information Systems (AMCIS)*, pages 149–155, Long Beach
           California, August 2000.

[RSL99]   Gustavo Rossi, Daniel Schwabe, and Fernando Lyardet. Web application
           models are more than conceptual models. In *ER Workshops*, pages 239–253,
           1999.

[Sch02]   Martin Schmidt. Design and implementation of a validating XML parser in
           Haskell. Master's thesis, University of Applied Sciences Wedel, Sept 2002.

[Sch05]   Uwe Schmidt. Haskell XML toolbox. http://www.fh-wedel.de/~si/
           HXmlToolbox/, May 2005.

[SdAPM99] Daniel Schwabe, Rita de Almeida Pontes, and Isabela Moura. Oohdm-web:
           An environment for implementation of hypermedia applications in the www,
           1999.

[Sjö02]   Martin Sjögren. Dynamic loading and web servers in Haskell. http://www.
           mdstud.chalmers.se/~md9ms/hws-wp/report.pdf, Oct 2002.

[Spi92]   J. M. Spivey. *The Z notation: a reference manual*. Prentice Hall International
           (UK) Ltd., Hertfordshire, UK, UK, 1992.

[SR95a]   Daniel Schwabe and Gustavo Rossi. Building hypermedia applications as
           navigational views of information models. In *Proceedings of the 28th Hawaii
           International Conference on Information Systems*, pages 231–240, Maui,
           Hawaii, 1995.

[SR95b]   Daniel Schwabe and Gustavo Rossi. The object-oriented hypermedia design
           model. *Communications of the ACM*, 38(8):45–46, 1995.

[Ste05]   Wikipedia: Didacus Stella. Auf den Schultern von Giganten (on the shoulders
           of giants). http://de.wikipedia.org/wiki/Auf_den_Schultern_von_Giganten,
           May 2005.

[TAS05]   A travel agency system. http://www.lcc.uma.es/~av/mdwe2005/
           TheTASexample/, May 2005.

[Tec03]   Techtarget.com. Web Site: Definition (http://searchcrm.techtarget.com/
           sDefinition/0,,sid11_gci213353,00.html), April 2003.

[Thi02]   Peter Thiemann. A typed representation for HTML and XML documents in Haskell. *Journal of Functional Programming*, 12(4 and 5):435–468, July 2002.

[Thi05a]   Peter Thiemann. An Embedded Domain-Specific Language for Type-Safe Server-Side Web-Scripting. *ACM Transactions on Internet Technology*, 5(1):1–46, 2005.

[Thi05b]   Peter Thiemann. Web Authoring System Haskell (WASH). http://www.informatik.uni-freiburg.de/~thiemann/haskell/WASH/, May 2005.

[Tho99]   Simon Thompson. *Haskell. The Craft of Functional Programming*. Pearson Education Limited, Addison Wesley, Harlow, England et al., second edition, 1999.

[vI05]   Arjan van IJzendoorn. Tour of the Haskell syntax. http://www.cs.uu.nl/~afie/haskell/tourofsyntax.html, 2005.

[Web05]   WebEngineering.org. WebEngineering.org Community Site. http://www.webengineering.org/, August 2005.

[WR05]   Malcolm Wallace and Colin Runciman. HaXML. http://www.cs.york.ac.uk/fp/HaXml/, May 2005.

Bibliography

174

Index

++ (cons) operator, 40
→ (arrow) operator, 39, 41
. (dot) operator, *see also* function composition, 44
:: operator, 39
>>, *see* bind (in monads)
>>=, *see* bind (in monads)
λ (lambda), *see* lambda (λ) abstraction
$ (dollar) operator, 45
_|_ (bottom), *see* bottom (in Haskell)

abstract data type, *see also* **data** (Haskell keyword), 34
abstract interface
    design, 26
abstract page description, *see* APD
abstract page structure, 18
abstract syntax, 34
abstraction, 74, 84, 91, 100
access
    primitive, 27, 28
    structure, 26
actor, 140
ad hoc polymorphism, 47
adaptation, 18, 136
anonymous function, *see* lambda abstraction
Apache, 33
APD, 67, 92, 100
application
    web, *see* web application
application domain, *see* domain, application
approach
    functional, *29*
    model-based, 12
area (in WebML), 21
ArgoUWE, 28

artefact, 4, 5, 66, 67, 175
aspect, 6, 12, 26, *175*
associative, 44
attributed label, 57
authorisation, 68, 70, *130*, *175*

behaviour, *see also* dynamics, 66, 68, 87
behavioural, 14
Berners Lee, Tim, 73
bigwig, 32, 33
bind (in monads), 50, 51
bottom (in Haskell), 45
breadcrumbs, 125, *175*
Bush, Vanevar, 73
business logic, 145

call-back function, 32
CASE, 20, 28
CGI, 3, 25, 32, 167
class
    (in Haskell), *see also* type class, 47
    diagram, 14, 28, 74, 141
    extension, 48
    method, 47
collection (in Strudel), 25
combinator function, 30
composite pattern, *see* pattern, composite
composition
    of functions, *see* function composition
    of pages, *see* page composition
compositional query language, *see* query language
conceptual
    model, *see* model, conceptual
conceptualisation, 66, 73
concern, 161
concurrency, 32
conditional (Haskell function), 98, *101*